DEBATES ON THE FUTURE OF COMMUNISM

A FOREIGN POLICY RESEARCH INSTITUTE BOOK
This book is sponsored by the Foreign Policy Research
Institute in Philadelphia. Founded in 1955, the Institute is
an independent non-profit organization devoted to research
on issues affecting the national interests of the United States.

Also by Vladimir Tismaneanu

THE CRISIS OF MARXIST IDEOLOGY IN EASTERN
  EUROPE: THE POVERTY OF UTOPIA
IN SEARCH OF CIVIL SOCIETY: INDEPENDENT PEACE
  MOVEMENTS IN THE SOVIET BLOC
REVOLUTIONARY ORGANIZATIONS IN LATIN AMERICA
(*with Michael S. Radu*)

Also by Judith Shapiro

COLD WINDS, WARM WINDS
  INTELLECTUAL LIFE IN CHINA TODAY
  (*with Liang Heng*)
LIFECHANGES: HOW WOMEN CAN MAKE COURAGEOUS
  CHOICES
  (*with Joan Hatch Lennox*)
RETURN TO CHINA: A SURVIVOR OF THE CULTURAL
  REVOLUTION REPORTS ON CHINA TODAY
  (*with Liang Heng*)
SON OF THE REVOLUTION
  (*with Liang Heng*)

Debates on the Future of Communism

Edited by

Vladimir Tismaneanu
Senior Fellow
Foreign Policy Research Institute, Philadelphia.
Assistant Professor of Politics
University of Maryland

and

Judith Shapiro
Resident Scholar
Foreign Policy Research Institute, Philadelphia.
Lecturer in Sociology (Adjunct)
University of Pennsylvania;
Villanova University.

MACMILLAN

First published 1991

Published by
MACMILLAN ACADEMIC & PROFESSIONAL LTD
Houndmills, Basingstoke, Hampshire RG21 2XS
and London
Companies and representatives
throughout the world

Printed in Great Britain by
Billing and Sons Ltd, Worcester

British Library Cataloguing in Publication Data
Debates on the future of communism.—(A Foreign Policy
Research Institute book).
1. Communism
I. Tismaneanu, Vladimir   II. Shapiro, Judith   III. Series
335.43
ISBN 0–333–53188–4

Contents

Contents

Notes on the Contributors

Humberto Belli – Former Sandinista and editorial page editor of *La Prensa*; director of the Puebla Institute, author of *Breaking Faith*, and associate professor of sociology at the Franciscan University of Steubenville (Ohio).

Mihai Botez – Mathematician and human rights activist in Romania; currently a guest lecturer in mathematics at Stanford University.

Aleksa Djilas – Yugoslav historian, political scientist and dissident writer; now co-editor of *Kontinent* and visiting scholar at Harvard's Russian Research Center.

Ferenc Fehér – Prominent figure in the Budapest school of social philosophy, forced into exile because of political harassment; co-author with Agnes Heller, of *Dictatorship over Needs*, and senior lecturer in the humanities at the New School for Social Research.

Carlos Franqui – Fidel Castro's former friend, a prominent journalist in Cuba before his break with Castroism; author of classic books on the Cuban revolution, including *Family Portrait with Fidel*.

Zagorka Golubovic – Former professor at the University of Belgrade; dismissed from her teaching post for political reasons; now a researcher at the Institute of Social Sciences in Belgrade and president of the Philosophical Association in Serbia.

Miklós Haraszti – Author of *The Velvet Prison: Artists Under State Socialism* and *A Worker in a Worker's State*, an editor of *Beszelo*, the journal of Hungary's democratic opposition. Currently a leader of the Alliance of Free Democrats and a member of Hungary's Parliament.

Agnes Heller – A leading member of the Budapest school of social philosophy; author of *Beyond Justice*, co-author with Ferenc Feher of *Dictatorship Over Needs*, professor of philosophy at the New School for Social Research.

Paul Hollander – Professor of Sociology, University of Massachusetts/Amherst; author of *Political Pilgrims, The Many Faces of Socialism* and *The Survival of the Adversary Culture*.

Jakub Karpinski – Former professor at the Warsaw University, lost his job because of involvement in the 1968 student protest movement; author of *Countdown*, a history of the Polish opposition; a frequent contributor to the Polish independent press.

Jan Kavan – One of the most active student leaders during the Prague Spring; founded the exiled Palach Press; now editor of *East European Reporter* (London) and vice-president of East European Cultural Foundation. Currently a leading member of the Civic Forum and a member of the Czechoslovak Parliament.

Edward Kuznetsov – Former Soviet dissident, spent more than 15 years in jail and was sentenced to death; author of *Prison Diaries* (winner of the 1974 Gallimard Prize in France) and *Russian Novel*, now with *Resistance International* in Paris.

Antonin Liehm – Former editor of a leading intellectual journal during the Prague Spring and now editor of *International Letter* (published in Paris, Berlin, Madrid, and Rome); his books include *Politics of Culture, Closely Watched Films* and *The Milos Forman Stories*.

Franz Loeser – Philosophy professor at Humboldt University in East Berlin; expelled from the university in 1982 because of opposition to the militaristic course of East German government. Author of *The Untrustworthy Society*, a critique of East German socialism.

Mihailo Markovic – An active critic of bureaucratic socialism, former editor-in-chief of *Praxis International* and author of *Democratic Socialism: Theory and Practice*; teaches philosophy at the

University of Belgrade and the University of Pennsylvania.

Carlos Alberto Montaner – Former Cuban journalist, wrote *Secret Report on the Cuban Revolution*; director of Firmas Press in Madrid.

Atanas Slavov – Former official of the Bulgarian Academy of Sciences, poet, novelist, and author of scholarly works on East European literature and culture, including *The Thaw in Bulgarian Literature*.

Judith Shapiro – Resident Scholar, Foreign Policy Research Institute; co-author with Liang Heng of *Son of the Revolution; Cold Winds, Warm Winds* and *Return to China*.

Aleksander Smolar – Polish political scientist who was one of the leaders of the 1968 student movement in Warsaw; now a researcher at the National Foundation for Political Science in Paris and editor of *ANEKS*. In 1990 he was appointed Special Advisor to Polish Prime Minister Tadeusz Mazowiecki.

Ivan Sviták – A philosopher whose ideas inspired the Prague Spring, he was stripped of his position at the Academy of Science. Teaching in American universities since 1968, author of *Czechoslovak Experiment*. Returned to Prague in 1990 as professor at Charles university.

Geza Szöcs – Hungarian dissident writer from Romania and activist for minorities' rights. Persecuted by the Ceausescu regime, he was allowed to leave Romania following Western protests. Currently a leading member of the Hungarian Democratic Union in Romania and deputy in the country's Parliament.

Vladimir Tismaneanu – FPRI Senior Fellow and assistant professor in political science at the University of Maryland; author of *The Crisis of Marxist Ideology: The Poverty of Utopia*.

Dorin Tudoran – Romanian dissident writer and editor of *Agora*, an independent Romanian cultural journal (published by the Foreign Policy Research Institute.)

Doan Van Toai – Former Viet Cong activist and author of *Vietnamese Gulag*, now executive director of the Institute for Democracy in Vietnam.

Jan Vladislav – Czech novelist and human rights activist involved in the Charter 77 Movement and editor of *Vaclav Havel: Living in Truth*.

Alexander Zinoviev – Renowned Soviet philosopher and novelist; author of *Yawning Heights*, *The Radiant Future*, *Homo Sovieticus*, *Communism as Reality*, and *The Hero of Our Youth*.

Introduction

The revolutionary year 1989 has changed most perceptions about the reality and the future of communism. Things that long appeared impossible – the complete collapse of communist parties in Hungary, East Germany, Romania, Czechoslovakia or Poland, the breakdown of the Berlin Wall and German reunification, the beginnings of multi-party systems in Bulgaria and even in the Soviet Union – all these have come to pass in less than 12 months. Those who make dire predictions compete with those in the throes of euphoria, but all agree communism is at a crossroads. The key issue is whether reform can cure systemic ills. Is the current crisis one that will lead to regeneration, or is it in fact communism's terminal stage? The velocity of transformations in East-Central Europe suggests that the evolutionary changes 'from within' have ceased to be the solution. In all those countries people consider the Leninist parties to be reactionary, and communism irrevocably bankrupt. But will post-communist societies necessarily be democratic? Or, rather, are we going to witness the resurgence of old political and ethnic animosities, long camouflaged by Marxist double-talk? More than ever, political traditions and mentalities, the content of what we usually call political culture, will determine the shape and direction of change.

For decades the advocates of communism maintained that their vision of social order was more just and rational than capitalism. Now even communist leaders admit that their record is deeply tainted. But this recognition was first advanced by clear-minded citizens from within the communist world. As we pass through the current crises, these are the voices that require the greatest attention of all: voices of experience, voices of prediction – voices from within. This collection of essays on the future of communist states is by authors who, by virtue of their birth, education and other biographical circumstances know communism as no foreign analyst or outsider can.

The multi-authored kaleidoscope we offer here requires a

willingness to shift gears to attend to the particular circumstances and viewpoint of each contributor. Yet the global reality of communism, with its multi-faceted nature, justifies the approach we have taken. The diversity of the voices in this volume echoes the immense diversity of the communist experience.

All of our contributors, including the American ones, have first-hand knowledge of the communist drama. What we have assembled is thus a record of both scholarly and political significance. It illuminates the major trends within the communist world, the scope and the prospects for the ongoing reforms, the varying role of intellectuals in political change in different countries, the ethnic tensions in the communist bloc and the erosion of Marxist-Leninist utopianism.

Our contributors come from a broad range of histories and experience in relation to communism. Some of them have actively opposed communism and suffered the consequences. As Jan Kavan, the former Czech student leader and member of Charter 77, a group dedicated to monitoring human rights, shows in his essay, the communist regime could not intimidate the Charter, which succeeded in irrigating the whole political culture and catalysing the coalescence of other groups. In the aftermath of the 'velvet revolution' in November 1989, the Charter's most celebrated member, playwright and human rights activist Vaclav Havel, was elected the country's president. In his essay, Eduard Kuznetsov, who was sentenced to death under Brezhnev during the suppression of the Democratic Movement in the Soviet Union in the 1970s, indicts the system for its corruption and anti-democratic features. These themes have in the meantime been adopted by Gorbachev's critics from the radical reformist wing of the Congress of People's Deputies.

Other contributors, such as Ferenc Fehér and Agnes Heller of the Budapest School, are anti-Stalinists but not anti-Marxists. They repudiate the bureaucratic dictatorship established in the name of the working class without denying the original Marxist project. For these 'revisionists', the revolution has been betrayed; a 'new class' – to use Milovan Djilas' classic term – has usurped political power and initiated new forms of exploitation. Publicly criticized in the 1970s for their humanistic stances, Fehér and Heller were forced to leave

Hungary in order to continue their theoretical inquiries. In their essays, these renowned social critics point to the role of society in the self-destruction ('de-totalitarianization') of the communist regimes. For them communism is a barbarous enslavement of the mind. To oppose it is a categorical moral imperative.

The Hungarian writer and activist Miklós Haraszti offers a pessimistic approach to party-sponsored reforms. For him, as for the Romanian poet Dorin Tudoran, communist governments rely on camouflaged violence, perfidy and cynicism. Can these 'values' underlie a superior civilization?

While some observers believe that communist leaders are taking dissidents' criticisms to heart, the celebrated writer and logician Alexander Zinoviev writes that the West's most dangerous illusion would be to take Soviet officialeze at face value. For him, the communist system is governed by objective laws such that even the most well-intentioned general secretary could not possibly transform it into a democracy. For Zinoviev, Gorbachev's spectacular rise to power is the triumph rather than the defeat of *Homo Sovieticus*.

Other critical intellectuals hold more optimistic views. Take, for instance, the members of the Yugoslav *Praxis* group. These distinguished Marxist philosophers started to criticize bureaucratic socialism in the 1960s. They saw their academic careers ruined simply because they refused to comply with the official lies. But, as Mihailo Markovic and Zagorka Golubovic point out in their contributions, socialism may not have exhausted its historical potential. For them, Gorbachevism contains a promise that should not be dismissed.

The reader will note that most of the contributors see really existing communism as a moral failure. To be sure, the East German philosopher Franz Loeser, who courageously praised independent pacifism and called for political democratization as a professor at Humboldt University, still thinks of socialist democracy as a political ideal. But events in that country have shown that this option is not embraced by the majority of the East Germans. As the March 1990 elections showed, the people of that country preferred reunification to 'socialist humanism'.

Almost all of the authors agree that communism is not

immutable. The Polish sociologist Jakub Karpinski, the Yugoslav historian Aleksa Djilas and the Czechoslovak poet Jan
Vladislav show that resistance to totalitarianism is possible. Without tremendous pressure from below, the Polish
communists would not have engaged in negotiations with
Solidarity, would not have legalized the independent union
and would not have accepted as head of the government a
Solidarity activist. The key to the Polish success has been the
revival of the civil society, the flourishing of an alternative
political culture where autonomous communication and free
initiatives can develop.

The special role of intellectuals in communist reforms is
discussed by Romanian mathematician and human rights
activist Mihai Botez, who analyzes the uses of nationalism by
communist parties in post or neo-Stalinist societies. Current
developments in Romania, Hungary and Yugoslavia show
that nationalism is definitely on the rise in Eastern Europe.
Antonin Liehm, one of the chief theorists of the Prague
Spring, describes the limits and the possibilities for
intellectual opposition to power. Another champion of the
Czechoslovak renewal, the philosopher Ivan Sviták, sees reforms
as a methodology of deception used by beleaguered communist
élites. His mordant assessment of Gorbachev's *glasnost* sounds
a disquieting note and should be carefully read. After all, it
was the Czech reformer Alexander Dubček who proclaimed in
1968 'communism with a human face'. At the same time, as
Aleksander Smolar and Paul Hollander point out, intellectuals
can take advantage of the new elbow room to promote changes
beyond the officially recognized borders of the permissible.

Through these diverse, stimulating and opinionated contributions, readers will get glimpses into the political culture
of such different communist regimes as Cuba and Poland,
Hungary and East Germany, the Soviet Union and Nicaragua,
Vietnam and Bulgaria. The book helps thus understand the
role of critical intellectuals in social activism. Theirs have
been pathbreaking efforts to create a space where human
beings will feel like independent subjects. They know, better
than anyone, that democracy is not a godsend and that
communist rulers will not simply relinquish their privileges.
The struggle will continue, and it will bring not only victories,
but also setbacks, sacrifices and disillusionments. As we see

in these essays, it now rests with civil society to become a counter-power, based on the centrality of the individual and the values of pluralism, democracy and self-government. While many of the forecasts advanced in these essays have come true, others have not. This points both to the limits of prediction in such an evanescent field as the future of communist states and to the need to further engage in such enriching debates.

The Editors
Philadelphia, 28 March 1990

Part I
Strengths and Weaknesses of Communist States Today

1 Communism's Strength: Democracy's Weakness

Ferenc Fehér

Had the question, 'what are the relative strengths and weaknesses of communism?' been asked fifty years ago, a likely and complex answer might have read as follows: in contrast to capitalism (which at that time was in the throes of predictably recurring cycles of crisis), the ultimate strength of communism resides in its vision of a planned and rational society. Irrespective of his admiration or contempt, the casual observer might also have pointed to the Marxist–Leninist ethos as a source of strength. Rightly so, for it created a unique modern type: the professional revolutionary, armed prophet of messianic expectations and self-sacrifice, expert of the technology of power beyond good and evil.

In addition to providing a template for the modern revolutionary and a model for a hyperrational society, communism at that time might also have been said to convey an image of a unified humankind. Half a century ago, one was presented with the image of the communist revolutionary who refused to acknowledge national affiliation, who remained impervious to the sentimental charms and unconditional imperatives of any national community, and who would acknowledge only one fatherland; 'the first revolutionary state of the proletariat', which seemed to transcend the limitations of the old European nation-state.

Amid all these positive features, one item would have figured prominently on the relatively short list of weaknesses: the insufficient industrial and military power of the USSR. Even this weakness, however, seemed to be a temporary deficiency, and would most likely have ceased to have been mentioned after the crushing defeat of Hitler by Stalin.

There is no need today to dwell on the obvious fact that history has made the items of strength and weakness which figured so prominently in the discussions of fifty years ago obsolete. If an inventory were to be drawn up now, a bottom line would quickly emerge: the strength of communism, as it appears in 'real socialism' today, which is to say in Soviet-type societies, does not reside in its doctrines, the practices it inspires or the system it is capable of creating, nor therefore in any of its inherent qualities, but rather in the various weaknesses of the democracies of other nations. The primary weakness of Soviet-type societies, however, is inherent in the system of communism and cannot be tied to external factors. This weakness may be located in the gradual erosion of the self-identity of communism.

What are the weaknesses of the democracies which indirectly bolster the challenge of communism, despite the latter's numerous fiascoes, despite the self-exposure by some of its own leaders (from Khrushchev to Deng Xiaoping and Gorbachev), and despite the worldwide familiarity with the image of the Gulag? 'The social question' is on the top of the list. Insofar as it remains unresolved, it may easily erode people's attachment to freedom. Although a society without some kind of unresolved social question is of course a chimera, its image nevertheless remains one of the problematic legacies of Karl Marx's thought. Marx tried to eliminate the dilemmas posed by the French Revolution by removing politics from his vision of future society and devising instead a 'metaphysics of the social question' which was to serve as a universal panacea. It is not thus the 'social question *sub specie aeternitatis*' that I would like to take issue with here as the main weakness of the democracies; it is not even, furthermore, the permanently conflictual cohabitation of democracy with the capitalist organization of the economy. Rather, I have several more specific issues in mind.

The first concerns the present systematic, theoretical and practical undermining of the authority of the welfare state. Although it has been justly criticized by the Left as well as the Right for many of its gross deficiencies, the welfare state is nevertheless the best answer to the social question which we have been able to devise thus far. A second point concerns the current morbid, indeed almost obsessive cult of economic growth, irrespective of its ecological or cultural costs.

A third weakness of the democracies may be viewed in the inherently illiberal and potentially totalitarian trends which intermittently rise to the surface. Hannah Arendt's famous distinction is crucial in this instance: the crowd, the multitude of citizens, can turn into a mob, a menacing aggregate of future petty tyrants and slaves, at those moments when these potentially totalitarian features surface. The recurring flare-ups of a latent McCarthyism, the organized hatred of those who dissent politically, the persecution leveled toward 'alien races' now so shockingly on display in France (which in its present language sometimes reminds us frighteningly of that of the Vichy government), are all factors prone to undermine the internal strength and moral authority of democracy.

A final weakness lies in the incapacity of the victorious democracies after World War II to devise a global system of economic management which rests not on the prerogatives of the stronger, but rather on the principles of social justice. After World War II there was a historic unwillingness, or perhaps simply a lack of determination, to create a global polity grounded in just peace treaties. This polity could have been based on the mutual respect of its members rather than on power or the mere rhetoric of the United Nations, which has become a caricature of unified humankind.

Any unbiased observer would have to admit that it is not solely or even primarily the democracies which must shoulder the burden for this political failure; the heirs of Stalin are in no position to teach respect for other nations' rights. Yet the painful but far from incidental fact remains that the system of Yalta, which was initially promoted by the democracies, was in reality an attempt by the so-called Big Three to construct a coercive world government. It is an equally painful fact that the concept of 'the free world' has itself for decades included not only genuinely free countries but also abominable tyrannies. 'The free world' was conceived as a system in which liberalism and authoritarian rule were to be merged under the banner of anti-communism. It was a system governed by the principle later spelt out, by Kissinger, in a secret maxim: security comes first, freedom afterwards.

The democracies have been paying a heavy price for this pedestrian Hegelianism in which unfreedom was paradoxically appointed to the role of the historical agent of freedom. They have been paying the price for this unholy alliance in the consequences of the Vietnam War, in the humiliations inflicted on them by the classic anti-Yalta revolution in Iran and in the ever increasing political problems presented by the unresolved question of German reunification. Unless there are some changes, the democracies will continue to pay. Recently, some promising signs have begun to emerge, primarily in the resolute support by the United States Congress for the democratic revolution in the Philippines and in the similar stand taken during the South Korean crisis. But these positions are only first positive indicators, and there has been no move as yet toward substantive strategic reconsiderations.

The ethos of democracy has undergone an equally deep crisis. The legendary slogan of the anti-draft protester reveals the depth of the decay which characterizes latter-day democracy: if indeed 'nothing is worth dying for', then the very idea of democracy – the Greek and Roman heritage upon which every attempt at *constitutio libertatis*, from the foundation of the American Republic to the uncorrupted days of the French revolution, has drawn – has become obsolete.

Communism, as it has been realized in the form of Soviet-type societies, offers no credible alternative to any of the 'democratic dilemmas' outlined above. Its record in solving the social question is appalling. Indeed, this record no longer satisfies even the Soviet leaders, who do not themselves suffer from unsatisfied needs. The totalitarianism of this form of communism is manifest and actual, not simply latent and potential. The order which prevails in the part of the world which is unified by the communist system rests on naked force and military occupation. Their ethos is epitomized by the 'socialist humanist' inscriptions which were found hanging on the gates of the concentration camps of the Gulag, or by the mob-like chauvinism incited by a power which proudly calls itself humanist and internationalist. Yet the Soviet-type system thrives, and will continue to thrive, on the structural weaknesses of the democracies. It is simplistic, as well as socially dangerous, to search for the invisible hand of the KGB (which is as active as the CIA, and perhaps more efficient), when communism seizes power on the unfree margins of 'the free world' or when the strategic unity of the democracies breaks down because of mass protests and counter-movements. For those who find democracy essential, even worth dying for, it is imperative that they realize that it is these structural weaknesses of democracy, and not some

communist or KGB-inspired 'subversion', which offer the
major source of strength for totalitarianism.

The inherent structural weakness of communism, on the
other hand, is revealed in its gradual loss of self-identity. It
may suffice to say here that ever since its historical emergence
as a political blueprint for action, communism has displayed
certain unmistakable and straightforward fragilities which
have helped to create its identity, irrespective of their 'apocryphal' status as far as the original Marxian corpus is concerned.
As a political blueprint, communism has meant the design
and the inevitably approximate, never fully-attained reality
of a politically and coercively homogenized society based on
universal control. In its ideal state, this society was supposed
to exist without any economic or political mediation. In addition, this political blueprint has also implied the politicization
of the entire network of social life. This has meant that communist society would not recognize or tolerate any distinction
between the private and the public.

In addition to creating a homogenized and politicized society, the political blueprint of communism has further claimed
a 'scientific' worldview which may be considered holistic in
the sense that it answers all the unresolved riddles of history
and human existence. This holistic worldview is by definition
so completely self-sufficient and superior to all competing
visions that the latter are considered superfluous, if not down-
right pernicious. Its 'dialectical' ethos, so rarely articulated in
an explicit manner, envisions the emancipation of humankind
through the complete subordination of every man and woman
to an authority beyond queries and appeals. This type of
authority is perhaps best exemplified by Dostoyevsky's 'Grand
Inquisitor', whose maxim of power consisted of the trinity
of the miracle (the 'substantive rationality' of the planners),
secrecy and the awe-inspiring prestige of the sword.

While the physical power of Soviet-type societies has
increased enormously in past decades, their self-identity
has suffered an erosion, occurring sometimes in a dramatic,
at other times in an underground, inconspicuous fashion.
The renewed efforts at socioeconomic reforms which have
occurred in the past decades do not necessarily affect the
political premises of the regime itself. However, even in cases
of minimal success, these attempts imply the abandonment

of both the ideal and the practice of the homogenization of a society based on control. Tacit popular resistance as well as the dissidents' inroads have posed obstacles to the efforts to make the private (even the most intimate) aspects of one's life public and susceptible to political control. In these cultures, 'human rights activism' consists for the most part in demanding the right to separate the private from the (politically controlled) public. This confinement of popular and 'professional' dissidence to the self-created realm of the private reveals both its weakness and its stunning success in helping to diversify coercively homogenized social space. Once superior, Marxism-Leninism as a worldview is now in a shambles. And no one shows more of a profound, albeit 'confidential', contempt for this world of science and philosophy than those who previously spread its wisdoms and who, of course, are still upholding its sway over cultural and academic life. In fact, it can be said that communism killed its ideology with its own hands, through its repressive intolerance of its own heretical branch: revisionist Marxism. Hegel was correct; only a Church which is capable of splitting and of coping with the split can hope to remain alive and vigorous.

Internationalism as an ethos died with Tito's successful nationalist revolt and Yugoslavia's secession from the regional superpower of the system of Yalta – with the direct or indirect Soviet military interventions against Hungary, Czechoslovakia and Poland; with the Sino–Soviet rift which at times has been played out on the battlefields; and finally, with the Albanian intransigence in the face of both the USSR and China. Wherever the communist apparatuses have had significant domestic support, this support has been nationalist-chauvinist in nature. Of course, one can continue to rule on the basis of this national tradition, but one can hardly hope to unify a worldwide movement with global aspirations by relying on it. Of the three principles of Soviet authority, the so-called 'miracle' (that is, the system's substantive rationality) has been discarded with the more or less public admission of the leaders that beyond a certain point the system does not work. If *glasnost* succeeds only to a limited degree, then secrecy will substantially weaken, if not disappear entirely. The prestige of the sword has to be aligned with the dignity of the imperial banner, that is to say, with 'patriotic tradition'.

The eyes of Russia-watchers are fixed these days on Gorbachev's 'restructuring' experiment, which has undeniably outgrown many of its merely rhetorical beginnings. True, its success or failure and the depth of superficiality of its changes will be critical political events of our time. And yet, for the leaders of Soviet-type societies, the greatest, most puzzling enigma is one which they are not likely to solve: that of their self-identity. The specter of what communism once was and has always aspired to be haunts present-day communism. And this unresolved puzzle will translate into acts of indecision, adventurism and false strategies.

This discussion is not meant to elicit what would surely be an unfounded optimism. Totalitarianism still has many options, each of which is frightening. It might fall back, for example, if only episodically, on the theory and practice of its classical period of a reign of terror. It might continue to survive as a totalitarian political (but no longer omnipotent economic) power which wants to prove its *raison d'être* by stirring up tensions and provoking wars. Above all, it could draw further strength for survival, recruit temporary zealots, and even experience further resurrections of its force and attraction, from its major source of strength – the structural weaknesses of the democracies. The conclusion of this train of thought is, therefore, that totalitarianism will not simply walk away from us. It can perhaps be substantially weakened, but if so, only through the acts of those who are courageous enough to live like citizens in societies which only tolerate subjects.

2 Sources of Strength and Stress
Mihailo Markovic

Before we can discuss the strengths and weaknesses of a large group of contemporary states, it is necessary to establish what characterizes them. They are not 'communist' because we call them that nor because their ruling parties call themselves that. Not one of these parties claims that it has so far succeeded in building a communist society. According to their own ideology, 'communism' is the project of a highly industrialized, classless and stateless society; they admit that they have not yet approached the realization of that project. Some claim that they find themselves in the socialist phase of the evolution toward communism. But since 'socialism' is used to refer to a mixed society, the definition is sufficiently broad to allow its application, with some reservations, to at least some of the states under discussion.

My reservations are that the idea of the liberation of the working class, which is essential in the entire history of the socialist idea, involves a level of political and economic democracy that is missing in those states; and that what we have in those states is a mixture not only of capitalist and socialist, but also of feudal elements.

There is also considerable diversity among those states, a consequence of the following four factors: first, the model called 'socialism' has been applied to countries at very different levels of social development, including industrialized and democratic Czechoslovakia; East Germany, with some industry and no democratic tradition; rural China; and all the gradations between them. Second, cultural traditions in these countries have been very different. Religion and the history of ethnic relations with Russia played a very positive role in the reception of the Soviet model by orthodox Serbs and Bulgarians and a very negative role with Catholic Poles. The attitude of Islamic people has varied between indifference and hostility. East Germans and Hungarians have manifested

10

the ability to resist but also to adapt – something they learned under the Prussians and Austrians. Another important cultural factor is the existence of excellent working habits in East German society as a whole and, to some extent, in Czechoslovakian industry and Bulgarian agriculture; these habits were comparatively inferior in other East European peoples.

Third, there were genuine social revolutions in some countries, such as China and Yugoslavia. The majority of people lent their active support and, even after many disappointments, they have not entirely lost their hope in socialism. This hope never had strong roots in the countries in which the new regime was imposed by the force of the Red Army. This especially holds true for Poland, Hungary and Romania.

Fourth, the socialist model was not applied everywhere in the same way. Soon after 1948, Yugoslavia abolished the *kolkhoz* system in agriculture, and introduced some elements of self-government, market economy and decentralization. In Poland the church played a significantly greater role than elsewhere, and large individual farms were tolerated. China paid compensation and managerial salaries to former owners of nationalized enterprises. Politically, Poland, Yugoslavia, Czechoslovakia until 1968, and even the Soviet Union under Khrushchev and Gorbachev, have been considerably more liberal than Bulgaria, Romania and East Germany.

In spite of this diversity, which precludes easy generalizations and universal evaluations of the present state of affairs in those countries, there are certain common characteristics which define the model and which, to varying degrees, are present in all these states. To begin with, there is a monopoly of political power in the hands of a bureaucratic party/state apparatus. There is hardly any area of society which can be characterized as 'civil society' in the sense of being independent and free from state intervention. Basic political powers have not been separated: legislative and judicial power are subordinate to the executive power, and eventually to the party leadership.

These political systems tolerate only one ruling party, which emerged out of a revolutionary vanguard of an essentially Leninist type. Only in Yugoslavia in 1958 was an experiment attempted with transforming the party into a primarily educational organization which would not interfere with self-government. The experiment was abandoned in 1972. Political pluralism is not permitted, not even in the more flexible sense of tolerating political organizations that do not compete for political power or try to get mass support for a definite specific political objective.

Also characteristic is that the abolition of private property for larger means of production gives the state a monopoly on economic power. In spite of the many differences in the amount of recognized elements of the market economy, relatively independent banking and the nature of planning, it is common to all those societies that the state retains the right to intervene in the economy at will. Also, some socio-economic rights are recognized and respected. The legitimacy of the state rests to a large degree on achievements in the area of social security (full employment, free education, free health service, guaranteed pensions to retired employees). Political rights are to some limited extent recognized but not fully respected. A culture has evolved in those societies that emphasizes social solidarity and elementary economic justice but stifles freedom of initiative and creativity.

In order to understand the possible strengths of these societies, one must not compare them primarily with other societies, but with their own preceding stages. With the exception of Czechoslovakia between the wars, the pre-revolutionary regimes suffered from different combinations of repression, corruption, stagnation, internal ethnic conflict and inability to defend their countries. Official ideology was able to claim that the new regime removed some grounds for widespread dissatisfaction: it could say, for example, that it destroyed a pro-fascist government or liberated the country. It led Russia out of an unpopular war, took the land from big landowners and distributed it to the peasants; in Yugoslavia, it gave the workers the right to run factories.

Until recently it was possible for these regimes to claim that in the entire 1950–80 period accelerated economic growth achieved the transformation of rural societies into medium-level industrialized ones. It is not clear whether the old regimes would have been able to attain comparable levels of development. Over the course of several decades, the people who live in these countries have witnessed a steady increase in their standard of living, and the regimes have succeeded in putting part of the blame for present difficulties on greedy foreign banks which extract huge interest on their loans.

While Soviet military intervention, especially in Hungary, Czechoslovakia and Afghanistan, has produced serious doubts about the nature of the Soviet use of 'proletarian internationalism', a good deal of the foreign policy of socialist states is accepted with approval by the majority of people in them, especially in the Soviet Union. To be sure, the situation is not the same in Poland and East Germany, in Hungary and in Bulgaria, in Yugoslavia and in Vietnam. Most people do not believe that the Soviet Union is likely to start another world war or to initiate a first nuclear strike against the United States. Especially the Russians, who lost 15 million lives in World War I and 20 million lives in World War II, do not tend to believe it. On the other hand, there is considerable sympathy for the support of liberation movements in the Third World. If there are mixed feelings in this respect, it is not because of fear of a Soviet empire in Africa or Latin America, but because it is ultimately the citizen who pays the cost of such ambitious military and economic aid programs.

When there is a tremendous amount of accumulated power in one center, it is possible to concentrate formidable means for the solution of any task that is perceived as extremely urgent: this could be accelerated industrialization; defending the country and winning the war; quickly building hundreds of apartments, as in the late forties and the sixties; constructing magnificent metrosystems; or making breakthroughs in space technology or nuclear armament. The price paid is the neglect of other areas. That is why so much Soviet technology, food and consumer goods are of inferior quality. Nevertheless, it would be dangerous to underestimate such a formidable rival and to believe that the system is in principle unable to deliver good technology or decent quality service.

These societies strongly support cultural development. True, they have resisted avant-garde culture for decades. Cultural policy concerning high art tends to be old-fashioned and conservative. It limits the full flourishing of culture by thwarting freedom of research and public expression. It is especially discriminating and repressive in areas that, by their nature, are close to ideology and able to undermine it: philosophy, social and political sciences, and, to a lesser extent, literature and fine arts.

Within these limits, however, culture enjoys high status and tremendous material support. Publishing houses, theaters and musical institutions are heavily subsidized. Thousands of scholars are engaged in full-time research. Education is free and offers one of the main avenues for social promotion. Although deprived of the advantages of free travel and first-hand experience of the world, Soviet intellectuals and youth compensate by learning foreign languages and reading more extensively than their colleagues in Western countries. They know more about the outside world than others, with the exception of experts, know about their own countries.

For ordinary people, limited culture is better than no access to culture at all. Mass culture for people creates a potential that can one day be decisive for social development. For example, the present-day flourishing of Soviet literature presupposes the accumulation of enormous quantities of previously unpublished work. The precondition for *glasnost* and *perestroika* was the development of a liberal spirit in the best parts of the Soviet intelligentsia, beginning with the thaws under Khrushchev and continuing behind the closed doors of private homes during the three post-Stalin decades.

The most basic weakness of existing socialist states is their identity crisis. These states pretend to be what a considerable extent they are not. Even many people who continue to identify with the system are more or less aware that there are enormous discrepancies between what the system actually is and what it ought to be according to the Marxist ideology by which it is legitimated.

The system was projected to be a network of 'free associations' in which 'freedom of each' would be 'the condition of freedom for all'. Some of the basic characteristics of the state, such as professional politics and institutionalized coercion, would wither away. Abolition of any exploitation of people by people would be one of the essential properties of this new type of society. Marx also believed that communists should not create their own party but join the ranks of the entire working class movement.

The single concept of Marx that was ideal for legitimating both Leninism and Stalinism was the 'dictatorship of the proletariat'. Using that terminology was the worst blunder Marx ever made. The 'dictatorship of the proletariat' meant workers' democracy for Marx, a state in which the majority population, workers, could rule. The dictatorship of the proletariat was to be a brief transition period, the purpose of which would be defense against counterrevolution and the restructuring of the economy. However, what was supposed to be a phase turned into a fixed system which continued to increase the power of bureaucracy instead of abolishing it. Probably the highest level of discrepancy between reality and ideology was reached when Stalin in 1936 described the Soviet system as the most perfect democracy ever to exist — just at the time when he embarked on a policy of mass murder of three-quarters of his own comrades.

One of the greatest mistakes committed by Khrushchev was the making of unrealistic promises, again widening the gulf between the real and the normative. In this respect, Gorbachev is much wiser: by seeking ideological justification in terms of Lenin's New Economic Policy, he decreases the gap and recognizes that after seven decades of building a 'classless, marketless, stateless' society, the Soviet regime is still in the initial stage of a mixed society, with strong elements of capitalism legitimate once again. This is indeed a right step toward overcoming confusion about the identity of the system.

A second basic weakness of socialist states is the political structure known as nomenclature. This is a hierarchical arrangement in which lower-placed cadres owe unconditional loyalty to higher-placed cadres, who, in turn, protect them and guarantee their future promotion. The principle on which this arrangement rests is typically feudal, reproducing under new social conditions the traditional relations between sovereigns and vassals. The nomenclature emerged out of the hierarchy of a revolutionary party, which, under the conditions of a politically repressive society, was compelled to organize in an authoritarian manner. Once in power, this party became the paradigm for the organization of the entire political society.

The type of bureaucracy produced in this way is essentially different from the Weberian-type of bureaucracy that emerged in Central Europe. Weberian bureaucrats are trained functionaries who obey the law and not any particular individual. Bolshevik bureaucrats are not specially trained; they occupy their positions on the basis of past merit and loyal service; they are not loyal to the laws but to the particular leader whom they follow and with whom they share their political destiny.

The system of nomenclature invariably led everywhere to the negative selection of cadres, to the elimination of independent-minded leaders, to the ascendancy to leadership positions of unimaginative, incompetent characters primarily interested in power and prone to corruption. No wonder Gorbachev had to start *perestroika* with a purge of such cadres. In this context, the rise of Gorbachev seems to be one of those historical miracles which demonstrates time and again that in every system there are rational human beings who are able to understand the perils of a degenerative trend and who may be able to reverse it.

The system of nomenclature combined typically feudal relations among cadres with a rigidly centralized organization of the state, economy, army and security police. The weaknesses of any authoritarian centralism are well known. Decisions about a concrete problem are taken at a great distance, in ignorance of its specific nature and of local conditions. Since the communication lines, all going from the periphery toward the center, are more or less clogged and the decision-making center is overburdened with too many issues awaiting resolution, decisions are often taken only after considerable delay.

A consequence of this kind of inefficiency is greatly reduced initiative at lower levels of the pyramid. The system does not reward bold initiative or prompt response to the challenges of the moment. Those cadres survive who patiently wait for directives, who are cautious, disciplined and as silent as possible. There is little chance that resistance of the apparatus will pose a threat to *perestroika*: once the policy has been changed, all comrades are eager to prove their loyalty to the new line.

A consequence of bureaucratic centralism is the low level of motivation it produces, with the exception of certain areas which have been given political or military priority, which may be well funded and supplied with the most creative cadres and best equipment. The most obsolete and least successful part of the economy is clearly agriculture, an area of production that responds least well to rigid administrative planning. The entire kolkhoz system is a definitive failure, in spite of enormous effort and investment. Even Gorbachev, who has for a long time been responsible for agriculture, first on the district committee of Stavropol and then as a secretary in the Central Committee of the Party, was not able to achieve any lasting success. He must eventually have come to the conclusion that the kolkhoz system will never function properly, and that nothing can be improved in agriculture without a resolute restructuring of the entire system.

The failure of the kolkhoz system has had very deep and serious consequences for morale. Anybody who has observed the poor organization of retail marketing must have wondered how it was possible to create such an efficient system of transportation and such an inefficient system of food distribution. The reason is not mere neglect in building enough department stores, but the fact that supplies of food are chronically inadequate to match the increasing needs and purchasing power of the population. This is the single factor that most demoralizes people and turns them into critics of the system.

The limitation of civil rights is a second such demoralizing factor. Waiting in queues every day for hours hurts Soviet citizens even more than the absence of political liberties. They withdraw from public political life, enjoy free speech within circles of close friends, and create a culture which is not immediately intended for broad public consumption but which makes their lives meaningful and which may be fully recognized in the future.

Nevertheless, Soviet people, especially intellectuals, will increasingly need greater freedom of public expression, travel, organization, political participation and communication with relatives, friends and colleagues abroad. That such need for greater political liberty exists has already been proved by the widespread support for *glasnost*, although one may wonder why this support is not even stronger than it is.

Socialist states are varied, complex and contradictory entities. They cannot all be evaluated in the same way, and none in black and white terms. Some of them are in deep crisis and sink deeper and deeper. Some are evolving and demonstrate a surprising level of vitality. The question is not whether they will survive, but how profoundly they will be able to transform themselves in the coming years.

3 From Paralysis to Self-Destruction

Carlos Franqui[1]

Communism's strength lies in its unlimited capacity for destruction, its weakness in its incapacity to construct and to create. In its first phase, communism destroys previously existing institutions, riches, culture and society. In its second phase, the terror associated with communism paralyzes political opposition, disobedient revolutionaries and individuality itself. In its third phase, the phase which prevails in the Soviet Union today, society is rendered incapable of rejuvenating itself, thus threatening by its very paralysis the material base which feeds its expansive empire. Communism has expanded greatly beyond its territorial boundaries, but it is immobilized from the inside by its fixation on the dominion of outer space.

The extremely difficult task which confronts Mikhail Gorbachev and his generation is not simply to modernize and democratize Soviet society but rather to increase its production of food and various capital and consumer goods. The Soviet Union has reached parity with the US in nuclear weapons and the dominion of outer space, but it cannot provide basic staples such as bread, beef, milk and wheat.

If communism may be defined as a movement which destroys everything but itself in its first phase and which paralyzes society in its second, then I believe in its third phase it will begin to self-destruct. Communism cannot coexist with itself. There are abundant examples of friction and distrust among communist states: the Soviet Union with China, China with Vietnam, Vietnam with Cambodia, and the Soviet Union with Czechoslovakia, Hungary and Poland. These fissures within the communist world do not imply, however, that it is incapable of advancing into Asia, Africa and parts of the Americas, to the peripheral fringes of the West where hunger, tyranny, dependency, frustration, injustices and endemic violence tend to create revolutionary situations which fatally degenerate into revolutions of the communist variety, such as Castro's revolution in Cuba.

Communism is in retrenchment in France, Spain and even Italy. It hardly exists at all as an organized party in Great Britain, Germany, Scandinavia, the US and other industrialized nations. I believe that an important factor which helps explain communism's retreat and retrenchment throughout the West is the contributions made to the public debate and the public consciousness by dissenters in communist countries, whose collective efforts expose for all to see and understand the numerous shortcomings of these societies.

Can a society which is unable to create, to edify, to produce anything, whether it be material goods or culture and freedom, a gigantic and omnipotent state apparatus which owns and controls all – can such a society survive? Can a repressive, unproductive, bureaucratic entity whose only weapons are terror and absolute control exist indefinitely?

Some ask why a society so brutal is incapable of engendering a political opposition capable of overthrowing it. The real answer, not easily apparent at first, is that in any country where the means of internal repression are debilitated by internal factors, or even by external factors on occasion, there have indeed been popular upheavals. Witness East Germany, Hungary, Czechoslovakia and Poland. In these countries, the Soviets have been obliged to intervene militarily using both Soviet troops and internal armies to restore order. Nor should we lose sight of the protests which have cost millions of lives in the Soviet Union, China, Central Europe, Vietnam and Cambodia.

In Cuba, after 28 years of Castro's communism, the revolution can only show the following: one million exiles; half a million victims of Castro's tropical gulags; thousands of deaths by firing squads; the longest jail sentences in history; a repressive apparatus numbering 500 000, including the army, state security and the national police; 20 000 wretched souls who have desperately escaped to freedom in makeshift rafts, many others having disappeared in the ocean and off the island's coasts; the destruction of independent trade unions, those very same trade unions created by the revolution; the annihilation of religion and culture; food rationing even for the most basic products; and the unencumbered, total control of all information and thought.

If it weren't for the opposition, if it weren't for the systematic protests and resistance, why would the terror and repression, draconian penal codes and proliferating jails be necessary? This is not the first time in history that a 'total' power holds sway over a people. Witness Nazi Germany. Yet it is extremely important not to lose sight of the fact that democracy has flowered in the most developed parts of the world only for a relatively short period of time. It is young, and more fragile than we suspect.

Today the Soviet Union, wellspring and model for the entire communist world, is not the country ruled by Stalin years ago. Even so, though the terror is less visible and brutal, it is still ubiquitous. In order to modernize the Soviet Union, Gorbachev must open his stagnant society. As he does so, contradictions will rise. These contradictions, by nature ineluctable, may lead to a reduction of his real power. This reduction may postpone reform, but the system is so devoid of dynamism that those who follow will have to tread similar paths.

Gorbachev is not a democrat. He is a communist who, under the guidance of the party and the state, would like to modernize the Soviet Union in order to make it stronger and more powerful. At the moment we lack sufficient historical evidence to predict whether he will be successful or not. But there is an abundance of historical evidence which suggests that, up to now, the Soviet system has been unable to reform itself, either from the top by the party leadership, or from the bottom by the people.

The modernization scheme proposed by Gorbachev brings a ray of hope, but it also poses a good deal of danger. If Soviet society does not advance, then its contradictions cannot be exposed. Yet it is these very contradictions that have impeded solutions to the most fundamental problems affecting human life, as the Soviet press itself has implicitly been informing readers in recent months.

If, somehow, Gorbachev were able to modernize the Soviet Union without having to reform it, this would be a grave peril for the entire world. Without a process such as the one he has embarked upon, dissent and opposition, symbols of the aspirations of the people, will be practically impossible, and without dissent and opposition, the creation of new institutions capable of altering the system are unlikely.

Contemporary history demonstrates that the communist system can transform itself into an industrial giant and military power by virtue of the slave labor it can harness. In the smaller countries, however, communism cannot aspire to even this tragic destiny. These countries have little choice but to become miserable Soviet colonies, which explains the evolution of Cuba and Vietnam into belligerent military states capable of fighting and winning wars for the Soviet metropolis.

Castro's strength lies in his marriage to the Soviets and the Soviet model, to which he has grafted elements of nationalism, caudillism, and homegrown revolution, converting Cuba into the repressive, unproductive monster that it is today. Castro's Machiavellian theory is that the small shall grow by leaps and bounds if they have a great and visible enemy such as the US to use as a whipping boy, especially if they have a powerful ally such as the Soviet Union. From this reality we can explain his attempts to export revolution into Angola, Ethiopia, Nicaragua and other countries.

Castro's strength is simultaneously his weakness. He is strong and enduring because he plays the Soviet card, but this is precisely what will destroy him. Since his system does not produce or create, the situation in Cuba, as in other communist countries, is deteriorating. Castro the caudillo has ruined the island. Where Cuba's presence is felt, the Soviets reap the spoils.

The post-Castro period will be an inevitable consequence of Cuban reality. Inside Cuba today there is a Hungary, a Poland and a Czechoslovakia. Even if Castro would prefer an apocalypse, or the transformation of Cuba into the Albania of the Caribbean, the seeds of liberty grow in the island and neither the Red Army nor Cuba's pervasive security apparatus can stifle such sentiments.

It is not mere wishful thinking to say that Cuba may someday be the first country to shake off the communist yoke.

NOTE

1.   Translated by Alex Rivero.

4 Sandinismo and War: Dynamics of Militarism in Revolutionary Nicaragua

Humberto Belli

Ever since the Sandinista revolution triumphed on 19 July 1979, the intentions of its leaders, as well as the dynamics of its political process, have been the subject of considerable controversy. While in the eyes of some observers the Sandinistas were clearly Communists, to others they appeared as revolutionaries embracing a novel blend of Marxist and Christian values.

Eight years later the view of the Sandinistas as Marxist-Leninist has come to prevail. The gradual disclosure of many of the Sandinistas' internal writings and speeches, their crackdown on dissent and their close friendship with Cuba and the Soviet Union have contributed to their characterization as communists or Castrists. Exceptions to this widespread awareness are still found among a few US scholars, as among some militants, church organizations and members of the radical left. It is very plausible, however, that in some cases such views are more the expression of disingenuous attempts at defending the Sandinistas before a rather anti-communist audience that of genuine convictions about the uniqueness of the Nicaraguan revolutionaries.

In this regard, Donald C. Hodges, a well qualified scholar who has provided the most comprehensive study of the Sandinistas' ideological roots from the perspective of the left, makes this observation:

> Although there are as many different roads to socialism as there are separate national states, the important point is that they are headed in the same general direction. Those

North American scholars who look askance at the Soviet Union while insisting that the Nicaraguan Revolution is unique because of its political pluralism and a mixed economy are apt to forget that a multiparty system is also a feature of such Soviet-bloc countries as the German Democratic Republic and Czechoslovakia as well as Poland. A small but significant capitalist sector survives in several of those countries, including Yugoslavia, which makes them mixed economies also. Thus Nicaragua already shares features common to these kindred revolutions in Eastern Europe.[1]

Yet, even among those who categorize the Sandinistas as communists or Marxist-Leninists, uncertainty still exists in regard to their flexibility or pragmatism, their susceptibility to influence, and their capacity to change or accommodate their course in view of adverse circumstances.

The round of peace negotiations, sparked by the so-called Esquipulas agreement of August 1987, (or the Arias plan) has brought a renewed relevance to questions such as: can the Sandinistas settle for a Nicaragua more similar to the one-party-dominated but non-totalitarian type of society that we find in countries like Mexico, instead of following the Cuban model? Are the Sandinistas irrevocably committed to the construction of an expansionistic, militaristic and totalitarian kind of state?

It is obvious that for the Arias plan to work, the answers to the first of the two questions should be positive and the answer to the last one should be negative: such a plan demands from its Central American signatories the full restoration of freedom of expression, political pluralism and individual rights. The questions, then, are not only whether the Sandinistas are really willing to democratize Nicaragua, but whether they can do it.

To some extent, these questions about Nicaragua are similar to the ones being asked in relation to the Soviet Union's *glasnost* and to China's overtures toward free-market arrangements. How far can they go?

The case of Nicaragua, however, is compounded by what seems to be its greater vulnerability and by the belief that its Sandinista leaders are in a near-desperate situation which makes compromise and reform more feasible.

What can reasonably be expected from Nicaragua? What are the chances for meaningful internal reforms? It is now a commonplace to state that there are few things as difficult as the art of political divination. This analysis is thus not an attempt to present a certain answer but an exploration of some of the difficulties that stand in the way of such hoped-for changes. That does not mean that a positive outcome is excluded or deemed impossible. To stress the difficulties is a methodological choice that is meant to enlighten attempts to find breakthroughs.

A foremost obstacle to change and reconciliation in Nicaraguan society is the militaristic civilization that Marxist-Leninist Sandinismo has been building. By civilization I mean not just the sheer size of the military forces or even the amount of energy and resources devoted to war or defense, but the existence of an ethos, of a whole cultural-psychological universe infused by military values and attitudes. A problem with this type of civilization is that war is one of its integrative mechanisms: war, or the threat of it, becomes functional for the entire system.

The nexus between communism and militarism has already been highlighted by different observers of the contemporary scene. The roots of this phenomenon are found in Marx and Engels' view of history as the battlefield of antagonistic social classes. For the founders of 'scientific socialism', revolution and war were intertwined. Lenin, especially, was forceful in his repudiation of the pacifist claims of some socialists of his time, who regarded all wars as evil:

National wars against the imperialist powers are not only possible and probable; they are inevitable, progressive, and revolutionary. . .[2]

Ever since the Bolshevik revolution in Russia, one of the most striking commonalities of Marxist regimes has been their militarism. Although in some instances such an outcome may be seen as a response to perceived threats of foreign aggression, their motives have been more complex than that alone. Trotsky's attempt to build a powerful Red Army – a task that he considered the number-one priority of the revolution –

was also inspired by his determination to bring many dispar-
ate, potentially subversive or counterrevolutionary elements
in Russia into a disciplined unity that could serve as the
instrument of Russian policy with respect to international
communism.[3]

Stalin further militarized the Soviet Union. He was followed
by Mao in China and then by the host of revolutionary leaders
who sprang up in the Third World. According to contemporary data, of the various governments in the world that
describe themselves as Marxist-Leninist, virtually all have a
far higher percentage of their population bearing arms than
do their non-communist neighbors.[4]

An outstanding case in Latin America has been revolutionary Cuba. Castro rapidly militarized Cuban society, creating a
'territorial militia' of more than one million persons (out of a
population of ten million) and a regular army of 297 000 (Latin
America's largest). Although the huge size of the Cuban armed
forces was ostensibly for the purpose of defending the island
in the event of an invasion, the truth is that Castro has kept
an estimated 40 000 troops in Africa for the past ten years.

In this regard, the Sandinistas have been no exception.
Their call to create a huge national militia was announced
within the first weeks of their coming to power in 1979,
at a time when the revolution enjoyed the overwhelming
support of most Nicaraguans and Western nations. Before
the revolution was one year old, it had doubled the size of
the army that had defended the overthrown dictator Anastasio
Somoza. By November 1981, when the Contras had around
400 guerrillas, the Sandinista army included almost 40 000
troops, by then the largest force in Central America.[5]

By 1986 the Sandinistas had amassed a regular army of
about 80 000 soldiers in addition to more than 100 000 in
the militia. The important fact, however, is not so much
the cause of this military buildup – whether it has been
undertaken for defensive as opposed to offensive reasons –
as it is that it reflects the building of a militaristic society
with its own internal dynamics.

That war and military symbolism stand at the heart of
Sandinista Nicaragua is evident from a vast array of indicators. Even from the beginning of the revolution, its leaders'
propensity for military language and symbols was expressed

in a variety of ways. The name of the official Sandinista newspaper was – and is – *Barricada* (barricade). To make the title even more explicit, the logo of the newspaper carries a guerrilla fighter shooting his gun from a barricade. As in Castro's Cuba, the real leaders of the revolution are all 'comandantes' (commanders), neatly dressed in military uniforms – except when a public relations firm advises Nicaraguan President Ortega to wear a business suit during his visits to the US. When the government launched a literacy campaign in 1980, the students involved in the effort were organized in 'brigades'. Those who participate in the coffee or cotton harvest belong to 'production battalions'.

The military nomenclature has been pervasive. An analysis of the speeches of the comandantes will find a rather repetitious set of words such as 'battle', 'enemies', 'annihilate', 'defeat', 'crush', 'attack', 'offensive' and others like them – even when referring to agricultural issues such as 'offensive against waste'. When the comandantes address the people, the latter usually cry out 'National Directorate, we await your orders!' Even more striking are the elementary school textbooks where children learn to add by counting hand grenades and bullets. The Nicaraguan youth are subject to a constant routine of military parades and the shouting of military-political slogans, where cries of 'Free fatherland or death!' alternate in a chorus of raised fists with 'Here, and there, the yankee shall die!'

The most notorious monument the Sandinistas have erected in Managua since their coming to power is a huge statue of a worker brandishing a Soviet made AK-47 assault rifle. The defiant figure, pointing its gun against the sky, symbolizes the ethos of the revolution's leaders.

The Messianic, sometimes apocalyptic vision of world revolution that appeals so much to communists everywhere often finds in the comandantes some poetic expression. Nicaraguan Minister of Interior, Tomás Borge, frequently provides some of them:

New offspring of history are being born in the midst of grief, anguish and heroic splendor. Social revolution is the order of the day in Africa, Asia and Latin America. Central America is being rocked with social earthquakes.[6]

But the Sandinistas' imagery of conflict, war and revolution springs not only from their ideological roots in Sandino, Marx, Engels, Lenin and Guevara, but also from their personal life stories. From Carlos Fonseca and Tomás Borge, founders of the Sandinista guerrillas in 1962, to the other eight comandantes who make up the National Directorate of the Sandinista Front, all have been full-time guerrillas and conspirators from early in their lives. As high school and college dropouts, none of them familiarized themselves with secular trades, jobs or professions. Nor did they acquire training in running businesses or institutions – except their very peculiar guerrilla operations. From their adolescent years as children of predominantly middle-class families until their coming to power, most Sandinista leaders have been people with guns. Many of them have lived rather dangerous lives. Some of them have personally killed – as Ortega and Borge – during their insurrectional years. Some of them have experienced prison and torture. None of them, however, has lived, for too long, what may be considered a normal life centered on work and the family. They chiseled out an identity for themselves: the revolutionary hero, the soldier, the man-at-arms. As a youngster aspiring to emulate Christ may find in the crucifix he wears the symbol of his identity, Sandinistas find theirs in the weapons they brandish. Some Sandinista couples were pronounced 'married', during the war and its aftermath, 'before the revolutionary rifle'.

In these regards, the military pasts of many of the top Sandinistas leaders are more poignant than that of Lenin and even Castro, whose guerrilla war was briefer and less destructive. It took the Sandinista Front almost 18 years of struggle to come to power. In the process, at least half of the leaders who came to hold the highest ranks perished. From 1962 to 1977 joining the Sandinistas was pretty dangerous. The movement was an organization involved not in open political campaigns but in subversive, armed, underground operations. They scorned those who decided to oppose Somoza in the conventional political arena as well as those who, on the left, preferred to devote themselves to trade unionism. Hostility against open, legal political work or trade union organization among the Sandinistas was made explicit in the early 1970s, when Humberto Ortega (Daniel's brother and now Minister of

Defense) dismissed unionism as a part of imperialism's plan to promote a 'bourgeois democratic way out' of the revolutionary crisis. For them, legality meant co-optation into the bourgeois system. They saw in war and in heroes like Che Guevara a more attractive and dignified vocation.[7]

According to Casimiro Sotelo, the Sandinista Front's representative at the Organization of Latin America Solidarity in Cuba, the hope of the FSLN (Frente Sandinista de Liberacion Nacional) was to provoke US military intervention in order to further Che Guevara's call for creating 'one, two, many Vietnams' in the world, as a means of dispersing the forces of imperialism.[8] The Sandinista Front thus tended to attract those young individuals who did not feel put off by violence and war, but just the opposite. It became a meeting ground for many of those who either liked war – which is an ancient propensity among adolescents of many lands – or who were convinced of the redeeming and cleansing power of revolutionary violence.

The Sandinistas saw in the life of the guerrilla fighter the highest calling to which a person could aspire: to die as a guerrilla, the most glorious of deaths. 'One has to be like Che!' was the religion-toned utterance of Sandinista poet Leonel Rugama. Following in the footsteps of Franz Fanon, the Sandinistas were convinced that revolutionary violence liberates man from his hated bourgeoisness, allowing him to transcend his origins and become a new man. Comandante Omar Cabezas refers to his first combat:

> That was the first time I killed a man. I felt an immense happiness, like the tension of centuries had been released.[9]

When the warriors came to power, they were faced with a multitude of tasks for which they lacked the training, and often the inclination. They had to manage a badly battered nation, to restore the economy, to reorganize and to create several institutions, many of them civilian in character. They had to secure new credits, to renegotiate the Nicaraguan debt, to establish national and regional budgets. In a nutshell, they had to govern a country, not fight a war. And although they could frame these challenges in militaristic words, the new assignments were more prosaic and less exciting than the thrills of preparing ambushes and counterattacks.

Whoever believes that the Sandinistas chose the military road reluctantly, as the painful but necessary price of defending their revolution, ignores their most basic internal dynamics. The drive to create a militaristic society geared for confrontation was a more appealing option than confining their uniforms to the closets and taking up the humbler tasks of dealing with multitudes of insistent housewives and peasants, consumers and producers.

To be sure, the model of the military society fit their ideological makeup better. It readied Nicaragua to fight the arch enemy of all peoples, American Imperialism, and placed the Sandinistas in a better position to resist the unavoidable – and predictable – reactions to their determination to support their revolutionary brethren in Central America.

Internally, the advantages of this choice were multifold. The first obvious one the Sandinista leaders found in modeling Nicaragua along the Spartan rather than the Athenian model (using modern examples we could refer to a Cuban-type militaristic society compared to a Costa Rican-type civilian, disarmed society) was that this model better suited their personal identities. As heads of a society confronting a dangerous enemy they could reenact those roles in which they felt most comfortable. They did not have to change clothes or attitudes. They could avoid the boredom of relatively unexciting and routine civilian tasks and follow the call of duty in more glorious endeavors. War demands valor, courage, heroism and sacrifice, values that the former guerrillas revered most.

Another advantage was the cohering power of a state of war. As German sociologist Georg Simmel stressed, conflict has perceptible integrative effects.[10] It reinforces the feeling of community and helps to mend or prevent many fractures and divisions – at least for as long as the external threat lasts. 'Under the spur of danger ahead, of dangers and hardships faced communally in the past, of the fruits of victory won in common effort, and of the moral exhilaration that comes from achieving objectives in concert, the feeling of community can be very intense indeed.'[11]

It is also the case that the specter of war, real or imaginary, helps a regime to legitimize its claim on the unconditional allegiance of the citizens. For totalitarian states, this aspect has been one of the most attractive of all. The nation is kept in a state of constant agitation and mobilization, the constraints of laws are suspended, emergency measures can be taken at all times, dissenters can be crushed as traitors to the nation and failings of the economy can be blamed on outsiders. For a government like that in Nicaragua, which has tried not to portray itself as communist, the legitimizing of repression was and still is one of their most difficult challenges. Having a real enemy to fight helps to solve this problem – provided that the enemy does not become too strong.

Another extraordinary contribution of the military civilization to the ends of the totalitarian state is its capture of youth. (In Nicaragua 50 per cent of the population is under 20.) Since wars are waged by young people, a state of war entitles the state not only to mobilize, but also to confine and train its youth. The new generation is thus forcibly removed from the influence of their parents and can be resocialized into the new revolutionary values. Although many young people may resist these attempts, a good number of them find that going into the military is a respectable means of breaking away from the routine authority of family and school and the relentless monotony of work on farms or in factories. They also find in military life a higher degree of moral freedom and license. The military society also appeals to youth because it stresses values and qualities which are usually associated with young males: physical strength, endurance, agility, capacity for effective aggressiveness.

More than 100 000 young Nicaraguans are involved at any one time in military service. That is roughly 20 per cent of the economically active population. Their contacts with their families are severely limited, as such contacts give them access to news and input from the outside world – recruits in Nicaragua cannot listen to radios. Besides creating the ideal conditions for resocialization, these circumstances place a great limit on the possibilities of revolt inside the country, since armed upheavals are usually carried on by younger people. They also provide the Sandinista state with a very effective way of absorbing the high unemployment in the Nicaraguan economy.

On the other hand, it is indisputable that the state of war and the mobilization and disruption of many other societal

functions entail some costs. The economy, in particular, is
one of its first casualties, and the Sandinistas are paying
a high bill. What is more, the scarcity of food has made
the rationing card almost obsolete. The state can no longer
provide consumers with their allotted quotas. Yet even in
this regard economic hardship has some payoffs. People are
so busy searching for food in the black markets that they
can hardly afford the luxury of participating in meetings
and organizations. In contradiction to some common beliefs,
insurrections and rebellions do not thrive in populations that
are frantically trying to survive. Riots may eventually erupt,
but it is unlikely that people will become involved in concerted
actions.

As a conclusion, it is possible to state that the militaristic
nature of the society being built since 1979 is so essential
for the revolutionaries' goals, ideology and psychological
makeup that they cannot relinquish it without threatening
their foundations. Militarism in Sandinista Nicaragua is there
to stay. As one of the nine top comandantes explicitly admit-
ted, 'military preparedness and increased military strength
cannot be viewed as conjunctural [temporary or exceptional]
tasks: they are permanent tasks'.

How then can we explain the Sandinistas' willingness to
sign the Arias plan and make concessions such as the
reopening of the newspaper *La Prensa* in October 1987?
Possible causes could be an attempt to curtail support
for the Contras at a time when the latter appeared more
threatening – or that the Sandinistas fell into a diplomatic
trap. Whatever the reasons may be, if the thrust of the
present analysis is valid, the prospect of a further, lasting
democratization of Nicaragua is either very unlikely or it will
introduce serious contradictions and tensions. A free press is
highly dysfunctional in militaristic societies. The payoffs of
tolerating it are confined to the nonetheless important arena
of international opinion where, as Marxists well know, wars
can be won or lost. And indeed, at the present juncture, the
need to appease international public opinion is a survival
imperative for the Sandinistas. Whether they will be able to
cope with this challenge without jeopardizing their own nature
is a puzzling question: warrior states are very reluctant to turn
their swords into plowshares.

NOTES

1. Donald C. Hodges, *Intellectual Foundations of the Nicaraguan Revolution* (University of Texas Press, 1986), p. 295.
2. Quoted in Robert Nisbet, *The Social Philosophers*, Crowel (New York: 1973), p. 87.
3. Ibid., p. 88.
4. James Payne, 'Marx's Heirs Belie their Pacifist Promise', *Wall Street Journal*, 5 April 1985.
5. Tracy Larry, *The Challenge to Democracy in Central America*, Department of State and Department of Defense (Washington, DC: October 1986), p. 20.
6. Tomás Borge, 'Women and the Nicaraguan Revolution', in *Nicaragua, The Sandinista People's Revolution*, Path Finder (New York: 1985), p. 46.
7. David Nolan, *The Ideology of the Sandinistas and the Nicaraguan Revolution* (University of Miami: 1984), p. 28.
8. Quoted in Nolan, op. cit., p. 33.
9. Arias, Pilar, ed., *Nicaragua: Revolucion – Relatos de Combatientes del Frente Sandinista* (Mexico: Siglo Veintiuno, 1980), p. 105.
10. Georg Simmel, *Conflict and the Web of Group Affiliation* (New York: Free Press, 1955).
11. Nisbet, op. cit., p. 14.
12. Luis Carrion, 'Is It Possible for Nicaragua to Defeat the War of Yankee Imperialism?', in *Nicaragua: The Sandinista People's Revolution* (op. cit.), p. 385.

5 A Dangerous Civilization

Eduard Kuznetsov

The ideas of socialism, founded on the notion that human reason is all-powerful, are to a considerable extent a heritage of the European age of Enlightenment. In that sense, socialism is the product of one of the orientations of European consciousness. As long as the ideas of socialism exist only in academic, armchair form, they appear quite normal, and may fairly be discussed equally with other ideas. As soon as they are applied in practice (whether in China, East Germany, Cuba or Ethiopia), a peculiar, strange and terrifying phenomenon occurs. In the essence of socialist ideas there is something which inevitably gives rise to a civilization whose principles are inimical to Western humanist culture and which at the same time differs in its essence from the darkest Eastern despotism.

Since it is not possible to describe all of the particularities of Soviet-type socialism, I shall consider only the question of how one of the basic claims of socialism came into existence, namely the creation of a new type of human being.

The preachers of the socialist revolution taught that the main thing is to get rid of the bourgeoisie, to expropriate them; with this will come the end of that notorious alienation and the blossoming of the human personality. The leap from the realm of necessity to the paradise of freedom will occur, and well-built, sun-tanned and joyous people will live in glass palaces, radiating love and kindness. Those who visit the country of 'real socialism', however, are struck by the gloomy faces of its inhabitants, their as-if-unmotivated irritability and readiness to engage in scandals and fights.

In 1979, in an article entitled 'On some Trends in the Evolution of Melodics of Russian Speech', the Soviet scientist Boris Gasparov wrote that the melodic qualities of Russian speech (the various parameters of tone, timber, tempo, dynamics and other elements that make up the 'unconscious' foundation of speech) have gone through fundamental changes in the past 60 years. Where pre-revolutionary speech) is

34

perceived as more 'dense', with a 'chest timber', the new speech is characterized not only by a higher but also by a 'lighter, more empty' sound. Gasparov notes that this 'suppressed' type of melodics was present in Russian speech before; however, its tense raucousness and touch of hysteria characterized only the tone of speech of the 'lumpenproletariat' and criminal elements.

One cannot but conclude that not only these criminal intonations but also a criminal psychology and view of the world predominate at all levels of the Soviet system. Most probably this happened spontaneously, because of the nature of the Soviet system. The latter has aimed from the outset against everything belonging to a higher order. To achieve the transformation of man into an obedient tool of the State, a man must be delivered of the ballast of religious faith and morals, and whatever is mean and self-debasing must be cultivated.

However, once the genie is out of the bottle, it is difficult to pacify him: by cultivating man's lowest instincts for its own profit, the system has to accept the inevitable losses resulting from general thieving and lying. Not only is cheating the State not considered reprehensible, but a person who does not do this is looked upon as stupid and worthless. One of the most terrible curses pronounced by the Soviet person is 'May you live on your salary alone!' Everything is organized in such a way that – as the proverb goes – 'if you don't steal, you don't live; if you don't cheat, you die of hunger'. Hypocrisy, theft and corruption are impossible to exterminate because they are inscribed in the Soviet system's genetic code, like the false tabulations which have become so widespread that it is impossible to believe a single figure provided by official Soviet statistical data.

The Gulag has played a considerable role in the general criminalization of the consciousness. Although at the present time, according to the estimations of Western experts, the number of people in concentration camps is 'only' about four million, there were times when the camps' population reached 12 and even 15 million. The Gulag is a real State within the State; at one time it even printed its own currency. In the USSR, everyone lives under the threat of the labor camp; the catastrophe can hit anyone at any moment. In the 70 years of

Soviet rule, no less than 200 million people have gone through the camp system, not counting the millions who died there. And most of them made the basic camp postulate their own, the postulate of the struggle for a piece of bread, for a space on the wooden bunk, for a breath of air: 'you go ahead and die today – I'll die tomorrow'.

The Bolsheviks knowingly used criminal elements both during and after the revolution, untying criminal instincts with their famous maxim, 'steal what was stolen!' However, although they nominated some former cutthroats and thieves to government positions, it is doubtful that the general criminalization was planned from the outset. They achieved this step by step, sometimes stumbling, but with inevitability. In due course, the regime realized the advantages of a criminal psychology and started to cultivate and use it.

Inside the country, this psychology is useful for attaining total control over all aspects of social life: if you take a mere nothing from your factory, your possible revolt is severed at the very root, your cry of protest will no longer bear that clear note of deep anger. You have now taken part in the general baseness, and your voice will tremble with falseness. The 'dense, saturated and chesty timber' will be replaced by the 'suppressed, lighter, more empty' sound. Besides this, criminal skill gives many advantages in the relationship with governments that still observe certain standards of internationally accepted behavior: it is no mere chance that one of the most important aspects of Soviet government activities is the systematic theft of Western technological innovations.

The fundamental sin of the Soviet system is not so much that to obtain a piece of sausage is a big event for some kolkhoz farmer, but rather that 'thanks to the constant concern of the party and the government', a power has been created which is peopled mainly by thieves, swindlers, liars and hypocrites. This is a power in which, as a result of alcoholism, close to 16 per cent of all children are now born with physical or mental handicaps; in which, according to official data, close to 37 per cent of the men are confirmed drunkards; in which every year 40 000 people die of alcohol poisoning. Vodka is the only consolation for the majority of Soviet people, including 40 million officially-registered alcoholics. Within an atheistic system, vodka takes on a mystical function, as it is a sure way to forget oneself and dwell in one's own paradise, at least for a little while.

And yet, despite the huge numbers of alcoholics and mentally handicapped people, one should not be deluded into thinking that this is a weak power. One of the hidden paradoxes of Soviet civilization is that although it is semi-indigent and drunken it is quite effective militarily. It is a military-aggressive civilization whose combativeness corresponds to the overall criminalized consciousness of its citizens.

People living under Soviet rule, the best representatives of whom were liquidated in their millions in the camps, have lost their souls, their beliefs, their moral heritage and their will to resist. Not only have they lost their own readiness for democracy but they also present a threat – through the fault of their rulers – to the world's free nations. That is why struggling for the freedom of enslaved nations is necessary not only on humanitarian grounds but also, primarily, on the grounds that this is one of the principal ways to ensure the security of democratic countries.

To conclude, I have a few words about the typical tendency in Western leftist culture to make distinctions between Marxism and socialism, and between socialism and the Soviet Union, and to analyze them separately. Defenders of this point of view say that Marxism is deformed in Russia because of the country's backwardness and the barbarism of its population. Yet wherever Marxism is applied, be it in a primitive African village or in industrially-developed East Germany, the results are essentially the same.

It follows from Marx' second thesis on Feuerbach that the question as to whether this or that type of thought corresponds to objective reality is not a theoretical question but a practical one. Therein lies the radical difference between Marxism and any other kind of philosophy, since Marxism is 'ante factum': it is verified in practice and only in practice. This practice, as shown by the 70-year existence of the first Marxist state, is truly nightmarish. Those who consider the country of real socialism as a slightly peculiar but essentially normal nation are deeply mistaken: alas, it is not.

6 Crocodiles Cannot Fly
Alexander Zinoviev

The seventy-odd years that have passed since the Russian revolution have been too short to draw final conclusions about the fortunes of the communist social system in general or of the Soviet Union in particular. Nevertheless, seventy years have been long enough for communist society to ripen and manifest its basic nature.

The weakness of Soviet society is its strength; its strength is its weakness. Do not regard this statement as a verbal trick! There is an old saying: our vices are the sequels of our virtues. The strength and the weakness of the Soviet Union flow from the same source: its social system. A given feature of this system can appear as a weakness in one situation and as a strength in another, depending on circumstances and the intentions of the leadership.

It would thus be a mistake for the West to base its calculations on some weakness in Soviet society. Many Western experts have pointed to the inefficiency of the Soviet economy – food shortages, catastrophic conditions in agriculture, technological backwardness, corruption, and so on. They see therein indications of the Soviet system's failure. Hundreds of 'prophets' have predicted the imminent disintegration and collapse of Soviet society from internal causes. Yet it stands firm. Western fear of the strength of the Soviet Union is equally misguided: the strength can be illusory, and what is often considered the strongest property of this country can prove its most vulnerable spot. In short, it is senseless to speak about the strengths and weaknesses of the Soviet Union in the abstract. Instead, one must pose questions about capabilities which can play different roles and reveal themselves differently according to concrete conditions.

Alas, it is not easy to understand the communist social system from a scientific point of view. Such attempts encounter resistance in the Soviet Union as well as in the West. The reason for such counteractions in the Soviet Union is obvious. The scientific description of the communist system is considered a slander on the social order. It enters into irreconcilable conflict with Soviet ideology, for the scientific approach discovers from the first step that real communism has little in common with the earthly paradise promised. The reality of communism does not abolish the social and economic inequality of peoples, social injustice, the exploitation of people by their compatriots or other defects of social interaction; it only changes their forms. Besides, it gives birth to new negative phenomena which have become eternal concomitants of communism. Although communism brings certain improvements in the living conditions of many millions of people, they have to pay for them with a new form of enslavement. It therefore goes without saying that the duty of Soviet ideology is not the unmasking of communism but the apologetics of it.

The situation in the West is, however, not better than that in the Soviet Union. Western notions about the Soviet Union are superficial and unstable. Various myths are fabricated which have nothing to do with Soviet reality. During the repressive Stalin years, the Soviet Union was held to be a paradise of equality, brotherhood, freedom and the like. The opposite myth dominated during the most liberal years of Khrushchev's leadership, when the Soviet Union was held to be a concentration camp. Now the West is seized by the delights of Gorbachev's 'openness', 'liberalization', 'democratization', 'restructuring', and the like. The efforts of critics to explain the essence of the system are ignored and the lessons of the past are forgotten. Soviet party officials are trusted more than those who have worked out a realistic understanding of the Soviet system, often at a great personal price.

There are many reasons for such a state of mind in the West, but I want to highlight the habit of examining the phenomena of communist society using the same system of concepts that one uses to examine similar phenomena in non-communist countries. For instance, concepts such as 'party', 'trade union', 'election', 'decentralization', 'productivity', 'private enterprise', 'market', and so on are used in the examination of communist society in the way in which they are used in Western societies. As a consequence, the Soviet Union is considered analogous to Western countries or at least to some Third-World countries. There appear illusions that the Soviet 'regime' can be changed by means of reforms from above, and changed in a way desirable to those influential in Western intellectual and ideological circles.

Western notions of the Soviet Union reflect not so much Soviet reality as the state of mind in the West. Actual, major traits of Soviet society are disregarded or underestimated, whereas imagined or secondary traits are scrutinized and exaggerated. The desired picture is projected as reality. The Soviet leadership organizes shows with the object of manipulating public opinion in the West; they are interpreted as a real re-organization of Soviet society. The West is eager to be deceived, but deceived in a way that is satisfying to it. The Soviet leadership has analyzed the psychological and ideological situation in the West, and now it supplies material for the Western mass media which feeds this quest for self-deception. Harmony has been achieved between the deceiver and the deceived!

Seventy years of experience of the Soviet Union shows that it is a mistake to consider the Soviet social system as a political body forced upon the population from above. This system is in fact a deep and stable form of organization of the people, who themselves constitute and uphold it. To eliminate it would utterly destroy the foundations of the entire society. It would take many centuries to change this system radically. No leadership, no party, no reformer, no pressure from without can abolish its objective regularities.

Soviet society overcame its adolescence under Stalin and entered maturity under Khrushchev and Brezhnev. It will exist in this form for ages if it is not destroyed from without. Of course, some changes are possible, and they occur regularly. But they do not change the social system or its basic laws. Gorbachev's reformist activity misleads Western people eager to be misled. But it does not transform the compulsory nature of communist social organization. Whatever the programs and intentions of the Soviet leadership, they cannot transgress the bounds of the objective laws of their society without catastrophic consequences.

Today's difficulties in the Soviet Union are not incidental, they are the necessary result of the social system. They are unavoidable consequences of the objective laws of the communist social order; as such, they are specifically communist difficulties. And they can be diminished and neutralized only by means which correspond with their social nature, that is, by communist answers to communist problems. These communist methods have been already worked out in the course of Soviet history, and their effectiveness has been proved. But it will take much time to overcome today's Soviet difficulties through communist methods. The leadership is afraid that there is not enough time since there is a threat of a new world war, and besides, they are afraid to use communist methods today, for they understand that their use will again expose the essence of the communist social system to world scrutiny. That is why Gorbachev's leadership is trying to solve communist problems by non-communist, Western-like methods which are alien to Soviet society.

However, Gorbachev's leadership is not really solving problems, but putting off their solution until some future time. New difficulties will appear as a consequence of such a policy, and the more successful this policy is today, the more difficulties there will be in the future. The imitation of Western models is dangerous and futile; the leadership's promise to raise the Soviet economy to a Western level of productivity is like the promise of an animal trainer to teach crocodiles to fly.

Part II
Can Communist States Reform?

7 The Paradigm of the Boots
Miklós Haraszti

In Budapest these days tourists love to bait their hosts with a question: is Hungary still communist? The tourists' problem is that they can't see where the system ends in this effulgent greening of ours; the hosts try to explain that under communism even the the grass is communist.

Spotting old structures amid change is the favorite armchair sport of masochists in my country – and I am a champion at it. I wanted to give you a lovely bouquet of the metamorphoses of communism. While picking it, however, I caught myself wondering why we must look for this weed once thought to be such an obvious threat to all other cultures. Are we heading toward an anarchist paradise in which I am an acorn, the state a chestnut, and we may grow alongside each other according to our natures? Or, will the meadow, in order to survive, require the communist state to carry out the only reform that matters – its own disappearance?

The question is useless. We don't need to ask it anymore. Nobody has yet seen a post-communist meadow. We might be able to imagine such a vista, however, if only we could figure out what the object of our concern is up to. But no one yet has been able to enter into a dialogue with weeds.

In Budapest there is an enormous public square adjacent to our equivalent of Central Park. Before World War II a church stood there, surrounded by trees. Bombs damaged it a bit, but it remained usable. Nevertheless, after the war the Catholic Church 'voluntarily' offered it to the state. The state at that time was an atheist one, and it proceeded to demolish the church. There were big plans for the site.

The area was transformed into an imitation Red Square. The trees were cut down, the ground covered with stone. Thenceforth on all official holidays hundreds of thousands of people poured into this plot. 'Working masses closing ranks', 'a flow of humanity surging and billowing' – that was our language lesson; and we thought if we opened our mouths to other words, they wouldn't be communism anymore.

But what kind of crucifix did they come up with for the Kremlin where the powerful lived, and for the Mausoleum where they lined up on the Founder's body to accept the greetings of their subjects? They solved that problem easily: they erected a giant Stalin. On official holidays, the Hungarian leaders would climb up to the bottom of his boots and wave down to the masses. The bulwark of power towered behind and above them, so they wouldn't forget that they were but governors.

It was designed to last forever; once a year a living flow of fathers would cover the square with the fathers of the future on their shoulders; in fact, we waved to Eternity itself as we marched in front of the Hungarian Father Number One, who himself stood in front of the boots of the Father of the World.

It was because of the failure of eternity that a school of thought insists that communism died on the evening of 23 October 1956. For it was then that workers brought tractors, cables, and blowtorches, and turned on the floodlights. While thousands watched, holding their breath, Stalin was symbolically lynched with cables around his neck. They exhaled as one man, in the world's loudest sigh of pleasure, when the statue fell, because they had done away with Stalinism itself. From then on, the history of communism turned on schools of interpretation, not just iteration of fact. The changes that began at Stalin Square would be used to illustrate the teachings of competing schools of interpretation.

For a few months, Stalin's bronze boots stood orphaned on the platform: a sculpture of tyrannicide. But already by May Day of 1957, the flow of masses billowed again. The boots were removed, and the reliefs showing happy workers were covered with red canvas. In later years the whole thing was smoothed over entirely with marble, becoming nothing more than what it was: a platform.

The fact that after the failure of the 1956 revolution no new statue replaced the old one shows, if you wish, that those in power had to retreat; their victory was Pyrrhic. Their setback was thought by some to be irreversible because though they now had to stand on the platform with only the weight of the phantom boots on their necks, in fact nothing was behind them but painful emptiness.

But isn't another reading of this emptiness possible? Perhaps our leaders found themselves some new form of legitimation, and their rule became even stronger. The fathers, with the fathers-of-the-future on their shoulders, were again ready for the annual march – this time without ideological slogans. Nor did they march, as in the past, out of fear. Neither their lives nor their freedoms are threatened if participants in today's parade don't attend. This annual pilgrimage is a respectable civil investment in their careers – and what society would morally object to that?

Such voluntary marching is regarded by optimists as evidence of a failure of communist power: see there, they've had to renounce total mobilization, to be content with their own true believers. The flow will shrink to a tiny stream as the number of genuine civilian activities grows, and with them the number of those whose happiness does not depend on the bosses up on the platform. Those bosses will have to accept this development because their economy will go bankrupt if they don't let well enough alone.

Well, perhaps. But until then – and for decades now – the masses continue to billow at the given hour each year. The megaphone voices can even be heard by the laborers in the exclusive casinos. And the megaphones still amplify the same martial songs that people never sing.

As it turns out, all during this time new plans were being considered for the platform. Which school of interpretation would be supported by this development? Did our leaders seek to escape from the memory of the boots when they decided to abolish the platform altogether and to build something else in its place? Or was it a sign of their reformist instincts that they considered demolishing the foundation of the idol and raising in its place the grand institution of national survival – the National Theater? This plan was apt because the much-loved previous National Theater had recently succumbed to age.

But then, what would have become of communism? Where would the masses billow if at all? Where would the leaders stand? Would the martial music cease?

The most intelligent part of the plan for erecting the National Theater on Boot Square was that everything was to continue as before. Only now, the leaders would conduct their official greetings from a special balcony on the front of the theater.

Our rulers were so pleased with this plan that they embarked on it in spite of a lack of funds. They thought to build the new theater and balcony with public donations.

Naturally, they didn't choose the slogan 'Buy One, Get Two'. They kept quiet about the balcony. But huge public enthusiasm was generated for the theater. In order to re-create the heady atmosphere of the nineteenth-century reform era, they issued building shares known as 'bricknotes'. 'Our Nation and Our Theater!' trumpeted posters full of palm trees on all the city corners. Why palm trees? You see, all bricknotes doubled as lottery tickets, giving donors the chance to win an all-expense-paid two-week holiday to Miami Beach – a place about as far from Boot Square as one can imagine. In addition, troupes of actors went overseas to rally enthusiasm amidst the Hungarian diaspora in America.

Again, we had reason to wonder what was happening. Was the Party admitting the fiasco of its communist values or was it simply (tactically) ignoring them?

The refugees of '56 might take satisfaction from all this. On the site symbolizing Hungary's colonial status, there would be recited the great lines of national dramas extolling independence. The victors were now pleading for the dollars of the vanquished. The leaders couldn't have devised a more modest retreat than to that silly balcony, which would remain, after their departure, merely a balcony.

But for the observer from inside, this is the story of stubborn continuity. The nation that felled the statue must now, if it wants a theater, build a rostrum for the same leaders. In what significant sense did the system retreat? Is it content to be reduced to a theater loge like royalty in a constitutional monarchy? Can it permit itself to retreat to such an extent that it will no longer be communism?

Or will it only rid itself of superficial elements and redundancies, in an effort to preserve the essential: the balcony? Why would it need the display of naked power, open terror, the ideological culture of the New Man – all once thought to be synonymous with functional communism – if the system runs more smoothly without them? Why can't communism embrace old cultures once thought to be hostile – like those of the nation and, yes, even money – in order to draw new strength?

You see, reform *is* possible. We don't need more daring changes than from Stalin to his boots, and from there to the National Theater.

But it is all the same. These 'changes' are simply variations in form of the same impertinent, self-congratulatory monolithic power. All this shadow play is really a paradigm of the boots, and while we are still inside that paradigm, there can be no real reform.

This debate can continue to the end of time.

P.S.: The following information might seem like an answer to the question of what will happen to us, but in reality it is just a corollary to the paradigm: there will be no National Theater built on Boot Square in Budapest. The leaders wanted to sell the public a plan that was too expensive. Not only did the Party not have enough money, but neither did the nation. So there remains only the old platforms, reeking of the old boots. On the site where they prematurely began excavations, communist grass will be sown to cover up the National Hole.

We may continue this game of tourists and hosts, interpreting the signs of changing times. But the collapse of the theater project is the collapse of the paradigm.

Maybe it doesn't matter anymore on what kind of platform our leaders will wave and smile.

The boot is inside us.

8 Toward Post-Totalitarianism

Agnes Heller

If reforms are defined as changes which are consciously and purposefully devised by political and social authorities and subsequently implemented by men and women subject to such authorities, then there is little doubt that communist regimes have always been reformed, are now being reformed and will certainly be reformed in the future. The more important question is whether or not communist regimes can cease to be communist as a result of purposefully devised changes in the social and political order which are implemented from above.

To further narrow the scope of investigation, we may ask whether or not communist regimes are capable of reform in this sense in countries where they are indigenous. This qualification is important, for wherever communist regimes have been imposed by foreign powers (for the most part the Soviet Union), the national issue overrides the sociopolitical one.

The first problem which must be elucidated, then, is what makes a regime a communist system *par excellence*? In the context of a longstanding tradition of political philosophy, I would initially place 'communist regimes' under the general category of 'modern totalitarian systems'. However, in doing so I propose to redefine 'totalitarianism', for its previous definitions were constructed when there was insufficient historical experience at historians' disposal.

Outlawing pluralism, but not abolishing it, appears to be the main characteristic of totalitarianism. The simple reason for this is that no modern society can exist without pluralism. Only an absolutely homogeneous society would be evidence of the abolition of pluralism and, contrary to what was earlier believed, viable modern societies can never be successfully and completely homogenized.

For the purposes of this discussion, I also consider it necessary to distinguish between a totalitarian state and a totalitarian society. A state is totalitarian insofar as political, but not necessarily cultural, social or economic, pluralism is outlawed within it. A totalitarian state might tolerate civil society in the capacity of a private sphere, for example, but it would never tolerate civil society as a public sphere, for the obvious reason that this would include the free exercise of political pluralism. According to this scenario, then, a totalitarian state does not recognize civic liberties insofar as they can be, or indeed are, publicly practised, but it may recognize certain liberties insofar as they are privately practiced.

A totalitarian state is invariably a single-party state in practice, although nominally this might be otherwise. As a rule, the single party seizes power in the name of a substantive value, rather than, for example, political and personal freedom. The domain of such substantive values may range from pan-nationalism to a centrally-planned society to racial supremacy. If the substantive value of the single party goes beyond the framework of nationalism, however, as a rule the totalitarian state established by this party will make attempts at totalitarianizing society as well. This attempt to totalitarianize society is tantamount to outlawing pluralism in the social, economic, cultural and other spheres, in order to reshape society according to the totalitarian party's blueprint. The 'blueprint' concept is especially important for understanding the totalitarian party's rationale. The criterion for the party's success is provided, and at the same time its place in the hierarchy of competing totalitarian parties and blueprints is defined in terms of the effectiveness of its particular blueprint.

A shift in the opposite direction, from complete totalitarianization towards partial detotalitarianization, can never be completely excluded because pluralism can be outlawed but never completely abolished. This statement is backed up by pragmatic evidence. As experience has shown, once pressure on civil society is eased even minimally, an allegedly extinct pluralism immediately begins to resurface. At such times, the direction of pressure is also reversed, so that it is now being generated from below. At these junctures, the ruling parties have three options: they may turn, in a complete volte-face, into triggers for detotalitarianization;

they may reluctantly cede to pressure, without genuinely detotalitarianizing general policies but with an increased tolerance of pluralism; finally, they may put maximum pressure on civil society in order to retotalitarianize the society and force the pluralist forces and practices back into their previous underground existence.

It may be a commonplace assertion, but it is nevertheless true that communist parties have always seized power with the intention of molding society according to their substantive blueprint. The common core of this substantive blueprint is invariably the doctrine of Marxism-Leninism, which can be combined with local populist or revolutionary traditions. The main features of the core doctrine include three aspects: the vision of a new social order, the means with which to achieve such an order and the tenet that this new order is superior to any others that have existed hitherto, particularly capitalist democracies. Owing to what might be described as the 'holistic-totalitarianizing' character of the blueprint, each of the three aspects assumes an equal weight. The substantive aim of abolishing all classes, social conflicts and money-based relations, and of establishing abundance and 'real' democracy, is combined with the abolition of private property and the market which, in blueprint terms, ensures the increase in productivity that will leave capitalist countries far behind. All this is tied up with the ruling position of the Party, with the 'dictatorship of the proletariat' and with the annihilation of the class enemies who are perceived as necessary for the functioning of the former constituents.

Today we are witnessing the fragmentation of this totalitarian blueprint. As a result of a great variety of factors, some of which are system-immanent and others accidental, certain communist leaderships have apparently lost faith in the feasibility of their original blueprint. However, no totalitarian political power can sustain a society in a state of totalitarianization *without* policies based on such a holistic blueprint; fragmented blueprints simply cannot suffice. The overall result of the present trend is thus a tendency toward the detotalitarianization of communist societies.

Although easing the pressure on civil society is the precondition of detotalitarianization, it cannot be construed as tantamount to it. Detotalitarianization begins when and where certain pluralistic tendencies in the sphere of culture, social life and particularly the economy are not merely tolerated but also legalized. For this to occur, the totalitarian party has to declare itself indifferent to ideologically sensitive issues and areas (for example, creative arts or religious beliefs) as well as to declare itself open to suggestions for rational policies in matters which need certain types of social regulation (economic organization, welfare, and so on). Decisions and measures which have been undertaken in these areas, as well as those which are pointing in this direction, may be considered genuine reforms aimed toward detotalitarianizing society.

The present assumption is that reforms of this kind are being initiated or reluctantly undertaken by the leaderships of the communist parties themselves. The reason for this change is that these leaderships have lost faith in the holistic blueprint, but not in their right to rule. However, this supposed 'birthright' to rule is itself inherited from ancestors who created and applied such holistic blueprints in a manner which left behind catacombs of victims and inflicted untold damages upon livelihood, culture and human souls. If, therefore, the Gorbachev leadership should one day recommend that the country return to where it stood in 1928, even the most naive members of a young generation might come to the conclusion that some 20 to 60 million people were eliminated in vain. They might equally wonder what gives such a party the right, apart from its sheer power, to initiate new experiments, after such a horrendous and costly historical blunder. Should such a 'public wondering' occur, then a serious legitimation crisis will certainly set in. Something like this has occurred, or is in the midst of occurring, in Eastern Europe. Should the communist leadership find itself reacting to this challenge with retotalitarianization, then the whole discourse of reform will collapse. There will be change, but not reform.

Is it ever possible to reform Soviet-type societies, as they now stand, in the direction of a non-communist system? One possible scenario is that no serious or profound legitimation crisis will ever emerge in these countries, and therefore the communist parties will be able successfully to steer a course of partially or completely detotalitarianizing society while keeping totalitarian political power intact. This scenario is far from being excluded, particularly in those countries which lack democratic or liberal traditions of their own. Would the surviving regime then be communist or not? Insofar as the ruling party continues to call itself communist, the term can still be applied, notwithstanding the demise of communist traditions; self-appellation is a fact of social significance. Insofar as the society emerging from such as identity crisis is no longer reminiscent of communism, even in name, then the term cannot be applied.

Another possible scenario might be that with the emergence of a legitimation crisis, the ruling party makes no attempts to mend and overhaul old blueprints, but rather conjures up a new or recycled one which is nevertheless holistic in nature. The new or recycled one could be completely different from Marxism-Leninism. It might contain pan-nationalistic or even racist or religious fundamentalist features. Once the identification of the totalitarian party with the new blueprint has been completed, it has a significant chance of partially or completely retotalitarianizing the society from the perspective of the new blueprint. This would thus be a reform of communism to a far greater extent than that conceived of in the first scenario, for under such circumstances these regimes would cease to be communist in any sense. Yet they would remain single-party totalitarian systems that continue to outlaw pluralism.

The two ways I have outlined of reforming communism are drastic, but neither points toward democracy. The first step toward democracy must involve the weakening or abolition of totalitarian political rule. At this point, the old Marxist-Leninist truth can be applied against contemporary Marxism-Leninism: ruling groups or classes do not give up their political power voluntarily. For this to occur, a revolution which is political rather than social is needed; there must be a change in political sovereignty.

It is not possible for political revolution to be carried out without either the use of force, which is the state of uprising, or the constant application of powerful political pressure on the organized centers of totalitarianism. The latter measure could occur without bloodshed, yet it would be a revolution all the same, for it could conceivably paralyze the ruling party to the degree that it would abrogate its total power. This scenario remains the only option for changing communist countries sufficiently that experiments with democracy can emerge. It then would depend on the maturity, wisdom and strength of the particular communist country as to what kind of democratic order it would ultimately establish.

9 Socialist Democracy: A Question of Survival

Franz Loeser

Mankind is faced with a seemingly insoluble and catastrophic dilemma: war, in the form of nuclear annihilation, leads to human extinction; peace, with its growing destruction of our environment, also threatens our existence. If neither war nor peace offers a valid solution, does this signal the end of human history?

In fact, this seemingly insoluble predicament is not an indication that human history is coming to an end but that the present social systems, Western-type democracy as well as 'really existing socialism', must prepare the way for greater social change than any history has seen before. In other words, mankind's prehistoric era is coming to an end and the dawn of true human history has begun.

Both systems have made immense contributions to this new era of human history: Western society with its ability to produce, its democratic heritage and the growing internationalization of economies, which is giving rise to a new internationalist-minded human being; real socialism with its attempt to overcome private gain as the motor of social production, its vision of a world without war, exploitation and poverty, and its creation of a new man and woman able to place the common interest of society before personal interests.

Today, not only the opponents but also unprecedentedly, the proponents of real socialism admit that the system has failed to fulfill its great vision. Is this because, as is often said, the egotistical, aggressive features of human nature can never be changed?

The truth is quite the contrary. It is not that the vision of this new man is unrealistic, but rather that it is an illusion that man or his society can remain as they are. If man is to exist in the future, he will not only have to change his society but also himself.

It is not primarily man's inherent natural weaknesses that have caused real socialism's failure to realize its vision of social progress. Rather, it is that this system represents a profound regression of social development because of its inability to change the Party's conspiratorial, militarist structure.

Without democracy, it is not possible to attain the measure of creativity necessary for a highly industrialized economy superior to capitalist society. It is not an accident that, for real socialism, democracy is a question of survival!

But is a system based not on private ownership of the means of production and production for profit but on state ownership of the means of production capable of democracy? If it is not capable of democracy, it is doomed to extinction. If, however, it can develop its own forms of democracy it may change the course of history.

To answer this question one must weigh the necessary conditions for democracy against the possibilities of change in this system. What are the mechanics of change? Do they allow for democratic reforms?

1. A people's movement must initiate and sustain democratic reforms.

Looking at the present Soviet system, there seems to be little scope for a popular mass movement for democratic change. Democratic changes are being initiated from the top: it is not the people but Gorbachev who is pressing for them. But looking more closely, one finds that Gorbachev's democratic ideas were created by the party leadership's realization that its political power was endangered by the failure of its economic system; and the failure of the economic system has ultimately been caused by the refusal of the Soviet people to work efficiently. In other words, the Soviet people voted with their feet, not as an organized movement but through spontaneous pressure, and forced the leadership to initiate democratic reforms. Similar developments can be seen in other socialist countries. This seems to indicate that even in dictatorial systems the people can, not only by open revolt but also through the spontaneous mass movements of inefficient work, force the party dictatorship to make democratic reforms.

2. The communist party must translate the democratic aspirations of the people into concrete political reforms.

Under conditions of party oligarchic dictatorship, the possibilities for democratic change are not only extremely limited, but the mechanics of democratic reform are also tremendously complicated. They are not, however, impossible. Generally the mechanics are as follows: the contradictions within society and the protests of various social groups are transmitted into the communist party in the form of differing and even opposing views among the party membership, giving rise, under certain conditions, to party factions. These factions, if deep and consistent enough, transmit themselves into the party machinery and even the party leadership (the Politburo).

The struggle among the factions within the Politburo will generally come to a head at the time of change of the general secretary, as is indicated by the changes after the death of Stalin or Mao. For the sake of strengthening his own personal power, the new general secretary must remodel his party machine, making it necessary and possible to change the party line. The changes may reflect to varying degrees the aspirations of the people, as transmitted through the chain of political power as described above. Especially favorable for such changes was the quick succession of three general secretaries after the death of Brezhnev. Gorbachev had an excellent opportunity to initiate basic changes. By this, we can see that there are possibilities for democratic reform even within the framework of a dictatorial system.

3. The dictatorial communist party must become a democratic party.

The source and repository of all political power in this system is the communist party. Only the democratization of this party can lead to a democratization of society. The Hungarian, Czech and Polish reform movements have shown real possibilities for the democratization of the communist party, which have been crushed or forestalled by the military force of the Red Army. These three movements have proven that the crux of the problem is the development of an inner-party democracy. There must be truly democratic elections of party officials and their possible recall; free speech; the possibility of political factions; limitations of the term of office for the leadership; and direct election by party members. However, inner-party democracy has so far not been achieved by any of the communist parties within this system. The attempts to liberalize the economy in Yugoslavia, Hungary and more recently China have already failed or are bound to do so if inner-party democracy does not materialize.

Liberalization without democratization is also doomed to failure. At present, Gorbachev has managed to carry out reforms in industry, science and culture, but attempts at inner-party democracy have failed or have not been attempted. The question, therefore, of whether the communist party can become a democratic party has so far not been answered.

4. The authoritarian and pseudo-scientific ideology of Marxism-Leninism must be overcome.

The necessary condition for democratic thought and practice is a democratic *Weltanschauung*. The Stalinist version of Marxism-Leninism, a crude perversion of Marxism, destroys every creative thought. Marxism-Leninism can be characterized as the conglomeration of three philosophical currents:

(a) dogmatic Marxism, which degrades Marxism to a closed system of absolute truths, the holder of this absolute truth being the party leadership;

(b) pseudo-Marxist pragmatism, which makes the criterion of truth and morality the political requirements of the party leadership;

(c) demagogical illusionism, which creates the fantasy that actual socialism is socialism, the highest form of democracy and freedom, representing the interests of the working class.

The main function of this ideology is to serve as an opiate for the masses and to ensure the glorification of the party leadership, crushing any form of democratic thought and practice.

Today, remarkable ideological struggles against the ideology of Marxism-Leninism are beginning to take shape in the Soviet Union. Indicative of this struggle is the attempted rehabilitation of Trotsky, the arch enemy of Marxism-Leninism. The ideological struggle centers on the following issue: was Stalin an evil tyrant who made certain contributions toward social progress, or was he a great statesman who made certain mistakes? The opponents of Stalinism, the supporters of Gorbachev, maintain the first point of view; the Stalinists, the second. The outcome of this ideological struggle is still open, but the fact that this struggle is taking place shows the possibility of ideological change.

5. The development of a democratic-minded citizen is a prerequisite for a democratic society.

In my own experience in East Germany, I was always struck by the puzzling fact that my colleagues were generally very fine individuals who were absolutely devoid of democratic ways of thinking. Yet how could it be otherwise for this generation who was reared in the Prussian tradition, educated by the Nazis, and made their careers under a Stalinist dictatorship? The conclusion could be that a dictatorial society such as actual socialism inevitably breeds only bigots. But this is simply not true. In every society the individual not only accepts the positive, but also revolts against the negative aspects of society. Historically, the growth of democracy can be explained as opposition to the totalitarian state. In the same way, actual socialism breeds not only careerists, opportunists and dictators but also democratically-minded individuals courageous enough to fight dictatorship. If this were not so, social progress would be impossible. So it is not mere accident but the necessary course of history that after a period of 70 years of Stalinist dictatorship a man like Gorbachev arises. I do not want to argue about what kind of democrat Gorbachev actually is – certainly not the kind envisaged in the Western world. Yet without question, Gorbachev has initiated a democratic process which can be temporarily slowed down or even crushed but in the long run cannot be suppressed. And it is beyond doubt that the limitations and shortcomings of Gorbachev's democratic ideas will be overcome and carried forward by future generations in Soviet society. This allows the conclusion that the rise of a democratically-minded individual, even in this dictatorial society, is not only necessary but possible.

In sum, after analyzing the strengths and weaknesses of real socialism it appears that this system is capable of rejuvenating itself on a democratic basis.

POSTSCRIPT: NEW FORMS OF DEMOCRACY?

My thesis raises a fascinating question: what forms of democracy are possible under conditions where the means of production are not in private but in public hands? Today we lack knowledge to answer this question adequately, but one thing we can say for certain is that they will not be identical with the democratic structures developed in the Western democracies.

Without question, these forms of democracy will have to utilize the positive features of Western capitalist society, but they will also have to develop their own forms more suitable for future development.

Future forms of democracy will be determined by the fact that the industrialization of material production will be completed and the industrialization of intellectual production will begin in earnest. Thus man will progressively be freed from physical labor and become predominantly a creative intellectual working in an environment of material and intellectual abundance. This abundance, coupled with the internationalization and computerization of society, will create a qualitatively new individual whose interests and aspirations will by far exceed the present intellectual level.

A parliamentary democracy, representing only a limited range of political interests and allowing for democratic decisions by the people only at certain intervals of time, will no longer suffice. It is imaginable that, with the help of an all-embracing international computer system, the new wealth of interests, needs, relations and contradictions will be voiced instantly and continuously by practically all citizens of the world community. Democratic decisions will be taken on the basis of the highest scientific knowledge for the good not only of the present but also of future generations. This indeed would pave the way for a level of democracy and social progress which represents the great vision of my Jewish forefathers: a world where the swords are beaten into ploughshares, a land where milk and honey flows, a time which concludes man's prehistoric era and marks the beginning of his new history.

10 Castro's Cuba in the Gorbachev Era

Carlos Alberto Montaner

All the symptoms suggest that Castroism is passing through a period of change. Such expressions as 'this has to change' or 'something has got to happen' or 'things can't go on like this' can be heard from many different quarters. I am not referring to isolated comments coming from people who are opposed to the regime but to expressions of discouragement made by individuals connected to the power structure – people who are close to Castro but who are aware that the decline of Cuban society in almost all its aspects has become intolerable. The most concerned and revealing voice is probably that of the former deputy economy minister Manuel Sanchez Perez, who defected in Madrid in December 1985. Among other things, he says that not a single one of the 50 ministers and 250 deputy ministers in the cabinet takes an optimistic view of the ability of the system to overcome the serious problems affecting Cuban society.

The desire for change is the first of a series of factors weakening Castroism. Castro himself is aware that the country wants and needs a change, but he can offer nothing better than an attempt to restore the collectivist spirit in accordance with the hoariest Marxist orthodoxy. For Castro, the only way out of the mess is to revive the revolutionary momentum and faith of 1959 and 1960; to this end, he started publicly in 1986 to criticize officials and administrators responsible for the most flagrant mistakes in the management of the economy. The trouble is that the punishment proposed by Castro for his most incompetent subordinates is not enough to appease the Cubans: after almost 30 years of dictatorship, very few of them believe the reason that the revolution is a disaster is merely because ten, a hundred or a thousand individuals are dishonest or inept. The consensus is that the problem is the system.

A second serious factor weakens Castroism: the economic crisis. The Castro regime has an unpayable debt to the West of almost $5 billion; it owes the Soviet Union more than $20 billion. Sugar, virtually its only export, brings on the international market only half of what it costs to produce; there is no way Cuba can meet its obligations, let alone pay its bills to the West. The country lives off Soviet handouts and it can do this only as long as the Soviet Union is prepared to continue subsidizing its remote Carribean satellite.

The third problem is the aging of the leadership. It is possible, even though it does not happen very often, for a people to love and support its leaders for a very long time, as is the case with Konrad Adenauer in West Germany, Urho Kekkonen in Finland and Luis Muñoz Marin in Puerto Rico; but for this to happen members of the government and the ruling class as a whole must demonstrate their efficiency and deliver on their promises. Adenauer, Kekkonen and Muñoz Marin all succeeded in developing their countries, in making the economy prosper so that in a single generation the societies they governed experienced a tremendous leap toward prosperity. There was no doubt about the relationship between their original promises and the results.

Fidel Castro, however, promised one thing and has achieved something quite different. Cuba has become a society characterized by misery, sacrifices and social tensions. It is legitimate to assume that disillusionment with Castroism is practically absolute; if this were not the case, we would have to conclude that Cubans are completely unlike other people on this planet. In fact, the leaders ruling Cuba today, having taken power 30 years ago, are perceived as elderly failures.

The fourth factor has to do with the wars in Africa. Cuban troops landed in Angola 12 years ago, making this the longest war in which any American army has ever participated. Moreover, the contingent fighting in Angola alone – leaving aside the units in Ethiopia – is bigger than all the combined forces of Fulgencio Batista, Castro's predecessor. Castro has had his Afrika Korps in Angola for 12 years and, according to general Rafael del Pino, who left Cuba in May 1987, this has cost Cuba's youth no fewer than ten thousand casualties. In Cuba itself, there are more than 50 000 deserters. Can there be any doubt that for Cuban families this bloody adventure is a source of irritation and tension?

The fifth factor is the coming to power of the reformist Gorbachev. This is an irritant not because the new Soviet leader proposes to make Castro imitate the Soviet model with its *perestroika* and *glasnost* but because Gorbachev himself has become an element spreading demoralization within Cuba.

His is the voice that cannot be silenced – even though interviews with and statements by him are censored. His is a voice which has, in indirect fashion, joined the chorus of those in Cuba, including Marxists, who are demanding liberal reforms to save the system from catastrophe. I am referring here to officials such as Humberto Perez and also the exhausted 'superminister' Osmani Cienfuegos, who would like to play at Gorbachevism if Castro would allow it.

Nobody should cherish any illusions about an ideological clash between Moscow and Havana. Like the Soviet rulers of the Brezhnev era, Gorbachev does not seem overly interested in the way the satellites handle their economies as long as there are no doubts about their loyalty to the Soviet Union and their agreement on international strategy. Be this as it may, Gorbachev has become the guardian angel of the fairly large faction convinced that Castro has led the country into a blind alley.

A sixth problem for Castroism is the absence of a true communist party enjoying real hegemony, which would buttress the system and underpin its authority at times of crisis. Castroism is paying the price for its *petit bourgeois* origin and the fact that the inner circle of power surrounding Castro was formed not by people drawn to the revolution for ideological reasons but by those who have attached themselves to the leader in ways that may be described in manuals of anthropology or sociology but are not mentioned in Marxist treatises. Castro has prevented the formation of a hegemonic communist party. A skeleton of one exists, but it has no more life than whatever Castro chooses to grant it. In communist societies, it is often said that people pass on but the party is immortal. In Cuba, it seems the opposite is true.

The seventh factor is the welcome existence of radio stations such as The Voice of the CID and Radio Marti, which reach the island with commentaries and reliable news reports. The current crisis would not be so serious were Castro able to concoct some alibi explaining it away, but these radio stations have made this impossible. Thanks to them, the Castro regime has been left without answers. They have snatched away his chances of producing a rhetorical rationalization of the crisis.

A stage has now been reached in which Castro cannot explain anything. He cannot blame anyone for the setbacks. He cannot defend himself with sophistries because the very next day the exiles' radio station would pull his arguments to pieces. This is serious for Castro because every system, even one with a million policemen ready to kill on its behalf, also needs political discourse. It needs an ethical framework to justify its behavior. Castro has lost this, hence his fury at these radio stations and his efforts to close them down.

I could list a dozen more factors that weaken the Castro regime, but I shall confine myself to mentioning in question form an eighth which is dictated by common sense: what would have happened in Hungary in 1956, in Czechoslovakia in 1968, or in the Poland of the seventies, if the Soviet Union, instead of being on the frontier, had been 5000 miles away with a wide ocean in between?

It is not at all hard to figure out the answer: these countries would have stopped being satellites. In other words, the geographical distance between Cuba and the Soviet Union is and will continue to be a factor weakening the Castro regime. The defenders of Cuban communism or, for that matter, its opponents cannot take for granted the inevitable presence of the Soviet Union simply because the Soviet Union is not in the neighborhood and could do nothing to prevent certain things taking place although it would undoubtedly try to control them. This geographical fact is the sword of Damocles which hangs over the Cuban–Soviet alliance.

Thus far I have been looking at some of the factors that serve to weaken the regime. There are others that tend to consolidate it:

The first and most decisive one is the determined support of the Soviet Union. Moscow's aid to Cuba has been estimated at $5 billion a year, a fantastic sum if regarded as conventional foreign aid but a pittance when you take into account the military advantages stemming from having an aircraft carrier measuring over 42 000 square miles just 50 miles off the US coast.

It is unlikely that anyone in the Kremlin would do anything to jeopardize the alliance with Cuba. For 30 years the Soviet propaganda machine has devoted itself, within the Soviet Union, to singing the praises of the Cuban revolution and to exalting the virtues of the 'younger brother' who in the Caribbean repeated Lenin's 'feat' of 1917. Consequently, it would be hard for Moscow to leave Cuba in the lurch. This would have a serious effect on Soviet public opinion, especially now that Gorbachev is going ahead with his half-hearted experiments in letting the people know what is happening and is, moreover, trying to strengthen his personal hegemony.

The second factor consolidating Castroism derives from reasoning by analogy: no society controlled by communists has ever been able to escape its fate. There can be no doubt that this fact serves to discourage dissidents.

The third factor may be the efficiency of the repressive apparatus. Nothing works well in Cuba except the legion of informers, spies and enforcers linked to the State Security, an organization spawned by the Soviet State Security Committee, the KGB. This is a formidable institution capable of drowning any conspiracy in blood. At any rate, this is what history has taught us so far even though the recent defection of intelligence colonel Azpillaga shows that even Castro's secret police is less monolithic than was once thought.

The fourth element comes from outside. The international community, including the United States, sees communist Cuba as a fact of political life that may be unpleasant but which cannot be changed. The United States, all of Latin America, and the rest of the West simply accept that the Castro regime is here to stay. This resigned attitude strengthens the system.

Also helping to consolidate the Castro regime is the absence of credible alternatives among the opposition. Time, quarrels and the genuine impossibility of doing anything in the short term – a clear detriment to political activity – have prevented the vast forces opposed to the Castro regime from presenting a solid resistance front that could be recognized as representing an alternative to Castro's government. This does not mean that there have been no efforts in this direction, but that around the world the public image of the exile is not very helpful.

Let us proceed now to consideration of some possible outcomes of the present situation. First, let us assume that the government rectifies its mistakes; Cuban society recovers its faith in the revolutionary process and there is a gradual reconciliation between the people and Castroism. The system is consolidated and the handing on of power without any traumas when Castro leaves the scene is guaranteed. In theory, this is not impossible. In 1956 Janos Kádár was the most hated man in Hungary, but more than 30 years later, he had recovered some of his prestige and managed to create under communism a society somewhat less dissatisfied with the system. Such miracles can happen.

But if Janos Kádár succeeded in restoring some of his prestige, it was because he was able to diverge progressively from the Stalinist norms that brought so much misfortune to the Hungarian people. Castro has taken the opposite course, choosing to crack down harder on discontent and press ahead with collectivization. We can therefore predict that the Castroite road toward the restoration of revolutionary prestige will prove counterproductive for the regime, that there will be an increase in tensions, worse economic failure and further demoralization within the power apparatus.

In a second scenario, mass discontent increases and work habits become even more undisciplined so that the economy deteriorates still further. There can be no doubt that this would result in more tensions in the power structure. It is there, in the economic ministries and within the bureaucratic structure as a whole where these things must be decided: however to further tighten the country's belt, where to cut back and where to take away. Economic crises mean less bread, less water, fewer schools, fewer medicines and so on, item by item right across the country's life. We cannot assume that communist regimes are immune to the effects of economic crises. The Polish government that preceded General Jaruzelski's was a victim not merely of Solidarity but also of the high cost of living and shortages. Much the same will take place in Cuba, and it is not inconceivable that there will be a new clash between Castro and the regime's reformist wing, which is getting steadily bigger and is concentrated in the administrative sector.

This is one of the hairline cracks in the Castro regime. On one side are those who know that the regime can increase its life span only if it introduces liberalizing measures in the economy and in public life as a whole. On the other side are those who think that liberalization would mean the beginning of the end of Cuban communism, because once this process was under way the capitalist germs would eventually devour the Castro-communist system in its entirety.

There is no basic contradiction between these two postures. Economic and political liberalization might enable the Castroite oligarchy to stay in power a bit longer, but in the long term an evolution towards a market economy and more democratic freedom would lead to the demise of the Cuban Marxist regime. On the other hand, were the Castro regime to retreat into a sort of bunker and dig in so as to fight against the inevitable, it might preserve its essential character but it would find itself up against the growing hatred of the Cuban people. It would be increasingly out of touch with the country's real problems, with nothing to look forward to but the definitive crisis. This could well arise after Castro's departure.

Another scenario cannot be written off: a military conspiracy is possible because Castro is leaving his own government clique with no alternatives. All those in a position of power know that were Castro to retreat into a bunker and cling to neo-Stalinism, whatever the cost, this would be equivalent to a death sentence for the system. Even if Castro should manage to keep power until the day he dies, the longer he lives the weaker his regime will be and the more vulnerable his heirs. If Castro insists on tightening the screws instead of loosening them, there is a genuine possibility of a palace plot. Cuba is full of generals like Del Pino and colonels like Azpillaga.

Let us suppose that the economic and social situation in the country gets even worse and that a group close to Castro, led, perhaps, by Raúl Castro, his very worried heir apparent, faces Castro with the need to liberalize the economy and relax political pressure. In this final case, Fidel Castro would probably be forced to accept his subordinates' line, but with a twist. He himself would not be in a position to propose the new course; he would have to change roles, perhaps adopting that of a living relic, uninvolved in the day-to-day problems of the revolution. Under these circumstances, Fidel Castro would reign, but he would not rule.

11 A Future Without Communism?

Ivan Sviták

Seven centuries ago a medieval monk invented a useful logical device called Ockham's razor, which posits that we should not introduce new concepts if we can explain problems with old ones – if a current theory offers a satisfactory explanation of a phenomenon, it is useless to introduce a new one. Since medieval monks are not among the favorite authors of the Soviet nomenclature, *glasnost* was born. We, however, can benefit from the old wisdom and avoid the clever ideological traps of *glasnost* and *perestroika*. These multilayered conceptual traps include the political trap for the middle class, which is led to support the shaky bureaucratic monopoly with the help of some intellectuals who would like to wear a roomier straitjacket, and the economic trap for the workers, who are supposed to accept abstinence and unemployment sponsored by Western bankers, as a new triumph on the road to communism. However, the most important trap is designed for the trusting liberals of the West, who are ready to cooperate in their own suicide. *Glasnost* is simply a sophisticated system of traps in which well-meaning visitors fall from one level of fraud to another, while they are offered an illusion of change. *Glasnost* is an ideology of reform without actual reforms, while *perestroika* is just the old Stalinism, polished on the surface to provide Western acceptance for the Politburo of Potemkins who are concealing the flaws in their imperial ambitions as skillfully as their tsarist teacher two centuries ago.

History has a different meaning according to where we have lived, and our views about the same events differ substantially according to whether we are active participants in revolutions, wars and movements, or mere observers. We also see the future in a different light if we know what a concentration camp is, prison, forced labor or exile, or if we have just enjoyed the fun of guerrilla war training from the comfort of our homes in the suburbs. Finally, our

answers are predetermined by our actions and by our willingness to commit ourselves to a project; pretended lukewarm
'objectivity' is only an academic self-deception. What is the
time in Prague? What is the Czech historical time? Knowing
that it is before midnight, should we, as exiles, capitulate
and modify our relations to the victor? Should we resist
with a feeling of hopelessness when confronted with the
avalanche of illusions provided daily by the media? We are
not living in Prague time, but we must resist because, for
an intellectual, exile is only the state of his critical thinking.
We understand our home better because we lost it: we
understand better, because the conflict of the superpowers
is underestimated in Europe and rarely perceived even by the
most enlightened Chartists. This is the strong trump card of
every exile.

In their modern history – and there is no other in the United
States – Americans have always been in an enviable position
because they did not have to ask strategic questions of history.
In any crisis, it was enough to mobilize the gigantic economic,
human and intellectual potential of the country and to solve
the crises of European wars or domestic troubles according to
the American will. If you can shape history, you do not have
any reason to respect it. The last two decades have modified
these American attitudes, because some have started to grasp
that the silent and anonymous powers of history are superior
to US military and economic might.

In the American public mind there is a deeply anchored
tradition of indifference toward foreign policy, benign neglect
toward the world outside US borders and willingness to grant
the benefit of the doubt to anybody who questions government
evidence. This attitude – expressed in the Roman principle *in
dubio pro reo* – has added to a basic ignorance about the criminal
character of the Soviet system. The occasional brutalities – not
limited to the Soviets – are not perceived as built-in aspects
of an oppressive system, but as historical accidents. However,
the real horror of bureaucratic dictatorships is not so much
in the rivers of blood and the heaps of corpses left behind by
the enthusiastic utopians, but in the fact that this system still
exists and succeeds. That should give the creeps to the most
optimistic liberals, but it does not; on the contrary, the most
modern system of oppression and exploitation is perceived

in the light of ideological myths about 'real socialism' which are successfully exported to the West, with vodka and caviar. This essential ignorance about the structural oppression in the Soviet bureaucratic dictatorship often leads to grotesque miscalculations in foreign policy and to a dramatic decline of American prestige abroad. The Americans see the Soviets in a more positive light than we, the exiles, simply because we are not impartial judges, we are eyewitnesses to crimes against nations and we do not have any doubts about the murderers. We cannot grant the benefit of the doubt to Soviet communism, because we have no doubts about it; it has been a criminal system all along.

THE STRATEGIC QUESTIONS

To answer the strategic questions about the future of communism means to clarify the role of the United States in global history. The first question – whether the communist states can survive – is central. My answer is unequivocal: yes, they can. An individual can live with a mortal disease for years, states can exist in decline for decades, and civilizations need centuries to collapse. History shows very clearly that the Soviet Union, that most perfect system of human oppression, has survived the gigantic crises of revolution, civil war, collectivization, deportations, mass murders, Hitler's invasion, Stalin's Gulag and the Cold War. The power élite was using a perfected system of terror for decades, despite its inability to feed the population. But Western governments stubbornly refuse to let the Soviet system perish from its incurable economic and political disease. Please, do not put the patient into an oxygen tank when he cannot breathe any more; do not give him financial injections when he is collapsing; and do not give to Ghengis Khan the newest technology because he starts to wear tailored suits from Dior. Please, please, please, let them rot in peace! That is my slogan for a new pacifist movement.

The communist states will survive because they have invented the most efficient system of oppression on this planet. Their gigantic disinformation machinery is capable of presenting their system as being a result of mankind's

progress toward freedom and wealth, when this is in direct
contradiction with the elementary truth. What is really shocking is that this terroristic practice works, that the population
can be forced to accept martial law as a normal condition
of life while Soviet propaganda propounds many reasonable
projects, attractive programs and global initiatives – despite
the fact that the government is doing the opposite. In the
1920s, the Soviets succeeded in convincing the world that a
planned economy prevents crises, although plans reduced the
living standards of the population; they pretended that they
found a solution for agricultural problems in collectivization,
although their policy caused famines and mass deportations of
millions; they adopted the most democratic constitution while
organizing pogroms of millions; they built 'socialist' society by
introducing a system of forced labor in concentration camps for
tens of millions, they claimed that they were the pillars of world
peace after they signed a pact with Hitler; and they claimed
that they reduced tensions through the largest militarization
in the peace-time history of mankind. If we know this, how
can we take seriously a program of *perestroika* without asking
what dark goal it covers?

The second strategic question follows from the first: can
the Soviets avoid the collapse of their empire, cultural decline
and economic backwardness by reforming the Stalinist system? If we mean by this term deep structural reforms of
the centralized economy and bureaucratic dictatorship of
a privileged ruling class (the nomenclature), then such a
change is impossible without a democratic revolution or its
equivalent. The state bureaucracy may try partial reforms,
but it cannot carry out serious ones for the same reason
that we cannot step over our own shadows. The logic of
Stalinist social relations is much stronger than the good will
to leave behind the straitjacket, which was the gift of Josef
Djugashvili to Mother Russia. If the process of reform were
to move far enough to scare the nomenclature – young or old
– then the 'sound core' of fundamentalists would be rallied to
push Gorbachev aside, as they did when Khrushchev became
too embarrassing. A joke from Prague states correctly that
there is no difference between Gorbachev and Dubcek, but
Gorbachev does not know it yet. The Kremlinologists who will
condescendingly laugh at the joke but who will not believe

the hidden truth in the joke – Gorbachev's built-in-failure – should be reminded that a theoretical analysis of this process was offered 60 years ago by Trotsky and 30 years ago by Isaac Deutscher. The practical efforts of the Berliners, Poles, Hungarians and Czechs, motivated by similar ideas of democratizing a Stalinist system, ended under the weight of Soviet tanks.

The history of communism does not know a single example of successful reform because no ruling class has ever given up its privileges without a fight. The new aristocracy of nomen-clature cannot democratize itself because its own system of privileges and the leading role of the police – pardon me, of the party – makes impossible any democratic pluralism of shared power or modification of imperial ambitions. Reform in the Soviet Union or Central Europe – if any – will be the result of a structural crisis of the system, of an internal, self-induced destabilization and unresolvable contradictions, not the results of the good will of individuals in the Politburo or of a reformist mood among intellectuals. Partial reforms for the worse, on the other hand, are probable, and the history of the USSR documents several changes in internal policy (war, communism, NEP, five-year plans, collectivization, and so on) and in international relations (Comintern, United Front, Hitler-Stalin pact, wartime alliance, Cold War, coexistence, détente). However, in no situation has the communist party ever dropped its claim to the leading role or ceased to pursue the goal of building the Stalinist empire. It is as paradoxical as it is true that the European left and the American liberals have each time welcomed the new party line, expecting a basic change for the better. This naïveté appears ridiculous to every émigré who knows the history of Stalinism, but not even a giant like Solzhenitsyn has succeeded in reaching the American mind with the simple truth about Russian reality.

The Soviets continue to suppress human rights but present themselves as the heirs of European humanism; they militarize their society in an unprecedented way but offer peaceful, even pacifist initiatives; they build their empire ruthlessly but accuse others of imperialism; they introduce new concepts of pluralism and democratization although the monopoly of centralized power has not changed at all;

and now, *perestroika* and *glasnost*, with their unknown content, are a source of hopes for an improvement which will never come.

Most Americans are not aware that the Soviet élite believes not in universal principles but in expedience in given historical situations. This is the main reason that there is a foolish belief that Soviet signatures on documents regarding peace, democracy, free elections or human rights express the same meaning as the Western words. The hypocrite lies as an individual, knows the criterion of truth, and acts alone; the ideologue is part of a state machinery and often does not know that he lies, because the criteria of truth are lost. The privileged bureaucratic élite believe that their lies are the truth they can dictate to history.

Knowing Soviet history, not just the distorted images which pass for truth, should we accept the Soviet claim that their system is a new civilization? My answer to this question is a strong yes, but we should also add that their civilization is worse than the old one, that *homo sovieticus* is a result of a historical malpractice and that all despotic regimes ultimately collapse because of their internal weaknesses. The barbarians who sacked Rome in 410 AD were also the representatives of a new civilization, or, according to the contemporary, Aurelius Augustinus, even the tools of Providence. It is quite possible that today we are facing a new dark age, and that after some three centuries of brutal practice, the Soviet Union will succeed in imposing its concentration camp model upon the globe. Its leaders are proud of their barbaric achievements, and they adhere to the goal of Sovietizing the world into a system of Soviet republics under their hegemony. To achieve such a goal, it is enough to limit the role of the United States in global policy, not necessarily to defeat it militarily. Then, in the new gulag civilization, the jailor can win the confidence of the jailed nations by making life within the barbed wire tolerable – he lives in the concentration camp too. Is this scenario just imaginative reporting from the deathbed of Western civilization? No, it is realistic, and has a historical precedent. When the barbarians crossed the *limes romanus* in 404 AD on their way to Rome, nobody opposed them because there were no legions to stop the invasion, while the sack of Rome in 410 was an absolutely unimaginable possibility.

The decisive problem for the contemporary West, especially for the United States, is to grasp the global competition of Western civilization with Soviet barbarism not as a question of atomic warheads but as a conflict of cultures. The *limes romanus* of ideas and the chain of intellectual fortresses must be strategically planned as a defense of humanist motivations, of critical thinking, as a search for the truth and meaningful human existence, not only in context with spheres of influence and zones of military operations in existing blocs. What separates us from the Soviets is their barbed wire, not ours, their Berlin Wall and their automatic weapons firing on anything that moves at the borders. The same devices separate the Soviets from Europe. However, the more relevant dividing line runs through the incompatible world views, philosophies, and value systems.

THE BRIDGE BUILDING BUSINESS

For the Kremlin's Politburo and for New York's Mafia, the final criterion is the practical outcome of a situation. Both the Politburo and the Mafia are based on a denial of the existence of moral criteria. History is the ultimate judge. If you are not caught, history has justified your action and moral scruples quickly evaporate. Anyway, who wants to correct history if the corpses are equally dead after rehabilitation? The Soviet communist party has ceaselessly and deliberately falsified its own history, because its leaders believe that history is 'the last court' of truth and if it justifies the outcome, the minor lies of the moment do not count. Lenin's testament was published with a delay of more than three decades, when it had no direct political meaning. Today, Leon Trotsky becomes again a real person after 50 years of deep freeze in Soviet history; when he became a non-person for Soviet public opinion, Stalin sent him a nice gift: an icepick which a hired murderer delivered into his genial head.

Soviet history must be constantly rewritten for every generation, and undesirable persons are removed from old photographs if they do not fit the new line. The current readjusted picture of reality, called *glasnost*, is only the latest distortion. George Orwell was one of the first Western intellectuals to understand that the fraud of Stalinism consisted in a rather simple idea: the Soviets were not thinking in terms of Western rationality and values, with a conceptual apparatus of verifiable categories, but they were and are constantly pretending that they do, knowingly exploiting the advantage which the open society gives them in the marketplace of ideas. What is shocking is the willingness to accept *glasnost* and *perestroika* as a new road towards the truth.

If that is the reality, what is the meaning of building bridges to the USSR? The bridges have led always into an open space, nowhere. It is useless to build ideological bridges to the Soviet virtuoso deceptions, to their Engelsism–Stalinism – but it is meaningful to sharpen understanding of the incompatibility of values in both civilizations and to recognize the truth about Soviet imperialism and about the brutality of their national socialism, which surpassed that of Hitler. If the Soviets want to be accepted as a part of a European tradition and Western culture, then it is up to them to see their own past critically. Can that happen? Perhaps. If Gorbachev succeeds in imposing a radical change of the party line, he could achieve in about a decade a deep change in Soviet thinking; then he could proceed from words to deeds. He could democratize the Soviet system and change the empire into a commonwealth of nations. Then the USSR would become an irresistible power in Europe and could win by peaceful means in a competition of economic systems. However, even if such strategic innovation were to become a party line for the rest of our century, I believe that the actual results would be unconvincing. The gap between the West and East has deepened and will continue to do so, despite the best intentions of Gorbachev's faction. In the new stage of global competition, the Americans could introduce a new system of social security, health care, economic democracy and job opportunities which would come close to the original utopia of communism – without sacrificing the freedom. The conflict of the superpowers cannot disappear, because the cultural barriers are too great; but the military aspects of the mutual threats could be reduced in favor of conflict of ideas and values. The nations could decide themselves. Whoever would win, mankind would win as well.

Paradoxically, the Soviets understand much better than
the Americans that the ultimate battle is the battle of ideas,
and they are watching to see whether the destructive power
of hedonistically-oriented culture and the power of crime,
money, drugs and sex will break the American mind more
efficiently than clumsy Soviet propaganda. So far, no superpower is looking for a 'historical compromise' – if we may
use Enrico Berlinguer's term in a global context – because
the conflict of ideas, cultures and values is dominated by
counting warheads, while most Americans live in a state of
holy apathy toward the role of the United States in the world.
The conflict between the Soviet Union and the United States
is not perceived correctly, as a result of Europe's collapse in
the two world wars, but as a moral conflict of good and evil.
The reasons for this conflict are believed to be a nebulous as
the chance to face the Soviets directly. My students do not
know words like Kolyma, Vorkuta, Katyn, GULAG, and they
have never heard about mass deportations, the Hitler–Stalin
pact or the Sovietization of Central Europe, although words
like Auschwitz or holocaust do appear even in the vocabularies
of the most academically disabled athletes.

Ten years after Yalta, Geneva or Helsinki, the Western
cosignatories of such catastrophies have finally grasped that
the 'free' elections in Eastern Europe were the opposite of
what was agreed upon in Yalta; that Brezhnev suppressed
dissent immediately after he signed the third basket from
Helsinki; and that détente helped to establish Soviet military
superiority despite treaties setting ceilings in the arms race.
The Soviets have never concealed their goal, namely the
growth of their empire, and openly declared that détente
was just a new form of class struggle; the other party in
the deal is not granted discussion rights, it just has to
accept the Soviet changing ultimata. The practical Western
politician is always ready to present some movement inside
the Soviet global concentration camp as a growth of freedom,
which curiously needs barbed wire.

Western players have been losing on the global chess board
for four decades, despite their economic and military power,
because the global chess game is not played according to
moral norms, nor according to the sophisticated rules of
diplomatic golf, where you just hit the enemy with a club

and wait to see what happens next. In a chess game, only a better mind wins, not a better manipulator of moves with the chess pieces. Western liberals do not know this and that is why they so easily accept the illusion of improvement now, when the Soviet Politburo is trying to satisfy some popular demands, hoping to break down the chronic apathy and the resistance to bureaucratic dictatorships. Will the West exploit the weakness of the opponent — as every chess player would do — or will the gentleman invite his counterpart to a golf party, at which they both will hit some third European party? Will the West offer financial assistance to the East again and reduce the self-defense by a kind of SALT III which will be soon regretted, when the enthusiasts for *glasnost* realize that the Soviets are ready to support the contracting party as a noose supports the hanged man — to quote a classic? Will American liberals ever grasp that it is time for intellectual disinvestment with the USSR?

In the global politics of superpowers, in which war and peace are burning issues, the bridge-building policy is the worst one because it is only a Munich policy, a strategy of concessions to the aggressor. For the Soviets, the simple flow of time is always creating new pretexts for violations of any treaty. History is superior to a piece of paper with signatures — how could it be otherwise?

Adam Michnik, the Polish dissident, recently stated that World War II did not begin because Germany had more tanks and airplanes than England and France — it did not — but because it had Hitler. This insight unfortunately appears irrelevant to the weapons accountants, who are playing global strategic games like the mere accountants that they are. It is irrelevant whether the Soviets have one hundred more or less warheads in one type of weapons or another, but it is very important if they have an aggressive goal or not. The Soviets have been successfully conducting a destabilization policy against democratic countries for 70 years, and the West is willing to write off its losses every decade. The international conferences served only to legalize, *a priori* or *ex post facto*, historical events and the growth of Soviet power. The victims of this policy — for example, one hundred million Central Europeans — were written off.

The United States is now facing the possibility of a débâcle comparable to Munich, Yalta, Geneva or Helsinki. If they sign a blank check for the spread of Soviet barbarism, then the AIDS of Sovietization will spread faster over the globe because the self-defenses of the nations will be paralyzed. The new Soviet attitudes and maneuvers in the Politburo are only a familiar movement of a pendulum which will start moving in the opposite direction immediately after new treaties with the United States are signed. Then *glasnost* will be recognized as a more aggressive policy, not a more conciliatory one, and the same people in the United States who were enthusiastically welcoming Gorbachev will be amazed by a new offensive in the Third World and by a new massacre in Central Europe, to which they have been already accustomed. How long did Khrushchev's policy last? The Czechs in Prague and in New York see *perestroika* with distrust, and they are referring to it with a similarly sounding Czech word, *prestrojeni*, which means changing clothes and presenting oneself under a falsified identity. Why? They had a bitter experience with their own bridge-building.

The Czech experience during the last half century is a horrifying warning for Western nations, especially in Europe, because in only five decades since Munich, a nation with a thousand years of European history, with Christian culture and democratic institutions, has lost everything and ceased to be part of the West. The voluntary and later involuntary Sovietization started with a bridge-building strategy. We should distinguish three different stages in this historical process of Sovietization of the Czech state, nation and culture, stages which can be repeated elsewhere. The first stage (1938–48) started with the adjustments made in foreign policy, in the fateful redefinition of the role of the Czech state on the European scene; this stage lasted about ten years and the goals were accomplished in a coalition of liberal democrats and communists. The second stage, lasting some 20 years (1948–68) involved the Sovietization of political institutions and economic structures and was achieved by the Czechoslovak communist party, under the strict or benevolent supervision of the USSR. The third stage, initiated by a crushing defeat of the democratization program in 1968, was designed to replace the national culture with a Soviet lifestyle, as a prelude to the incorporation of East Europe into the Soviet Empire.

The results of this Sovietization method were remarkably successful. In only four decades, a democratic state became a totalitarian bureaucratic dictatorship, humanistic Christian traditions were replaced by a cultural cemetery and a Western-oriented European nation sank to the level of colonial slavery. Soviet missiles with atomic warheads were placed on Czech territory in 1984. If we want to understand the causes of the present state, we have to return to that fateful December of 1943, when the Czechs signed a treaty with the Soviet Union. In Moscow the process of Sovietization of the Czech democratic state was initiated by liberal democrats, who gave a fateful impetus to the mudslide which soon buried them. The final conclusion is the worst: if contemporary Western democracies adjust their international policy to suit Soviet global goals, they will initiate a similar process which will bury their democratic institutions, independence and culture. Please, before you do it, check the Czechs.

Soviet Policy in Central Europe will not change with *glasnost*, because it has its deep roots in tsarist imperialism. The Russians were experienced in how to increase the pressure on small nations on their Asian borders, until the nations were incorporated into the Russian sphere of influence and occupied by military force. In the Soviet era, this practice of Asian Russification was adjusted to the new ideology, but it was not abandoned. In Europe, Sovietization became a colonization in reverse, because a less developed country was imposing its barbarism on more developed countries, proceeding with the forced denationalization of the occupied population because the local culture was incompatible with the Soviet lack of it.

Under these conditions, the primary function of the Czech exile must be a vocal resistance to the new Soviet strategy of *perestroika*, which does not change anything in Central Europe. The captive Central European nations have nothing to gain from Gorbachev's *prestrojeni*, because they are trying to get out of the nomenclature. They have no faith in improvement within the nomenclature, which ultimately will only increase the level of Sovietization. *Perestroika* is from their point of view doomed, because they have experienced what happens to reformers. When they wanted to increase the productivity of labor and tried to remove the inefficient old cadres, the unreformed Stalinists immediately started a counterattack, which was always successful in the long run. The Czech democratization was dialectically negated, with the help of some 500 000 armed Hegelians, and became a de-democratization, a restitution of a neo-Stalinist system. The gorillas in the Polish apparat have not hesitated to introduce classical Stalinist methods: concentration camps for the union leaders and martial law for everybody else. In the light of these experiences with reformism in Central Europe, it is naive to believe that the new Soviet middle class, with some intellectual help, will fare better than the Polish workers. Czechoslovakia had the strongest middle class, but even the Moscow-trained leaders, with powerful help from two nations, have not succeeded in reforming Stalinism, simply because no one can square that circle. Today, the Soviet nomenclature does not include only the top apparatchiki, it includes whole nations; the results of the Brezhnev doctrine were sanctioned not only in Helsinki, but also by Gorbachev during his Prague visit (in spring 1987). Thanks to their unique experience with different stages of voluntary and involuntary Sovietization, the Czechoslovaks see the Russian and the Czechoslovak communists as imperialist occupants, corrupt collaborators and tools of barbarism. The Czechs are rotting with the Soviet Union, and Gorbachev has only confirmed that the metamorphosis of Stalinism continues. Brezhnev's doctrine is his doctrine as well. Hence we Czechs do not care whether Gorbachev falls or remains; we are only interested in ending the policy of abnormalization, and in recovering some space for our own national culture. 'Mister Gorbachev, we Czechs do not believe a single word, but if you want to gain ten million supporters, withdraw the occupation army. Even the most skeptical voices will shout: 'Long live Gorbachev's perestroika!' With Gorbachev or without him, the Czech future is a future without Soviet communism, because with it we do not have any future at all.

12 Reforms Are Possible
Doan Van Toai

The Soviets have an uninterrupted history of conquest under
the banner of liberation and control under the banner of independence. Communist wars of liberation have succeeded in
the postwar era because the United States, the only Western
power that could have played a leadership role, ignored the
plight of the Third World. The key mistake of the West
after World War II was its unwillingness to support national
liberation movements. In case after case, the United States
either stayed neutral in wars of national liberation or took
the side of the colonialists.

This attitude played into the hands of the Soviets. While
the United States saw the world as divided into two camps, the
wicked communists and the freedom-loving anti-communists,
many of us in the Third World saw the division very differently. We saw on one side the national independence
movements in former colonies, fighting for their freedom with
the support of the Soviets; and on the other side reactionary
forces, unpopular, corrupt and supported by the Americans.

Western leaders failed to convince their people and the
people of the Third World that the communists were evil.
So, when the West became involved with anti-communist
wars in China, Vietnam and elsewhere, they were seriously
handicapped in the battle for the 'hearts and minds' of the
people in these countries. Independence was and is the most
powerful issue in many Third-World nations. Too often, the
people of those nations did not see their anti-communist,
often repressive regimes as steps in the direction of independence, but as a continuation of colonial control.

Moreover, the corruption and repression of these regimes,
together with their complicity with foreigners, deflected attention from the atrocities committed by their communist opponents. As one who fought against what I saw as the imperialist American presence in my country, I can say that my
compatriots and I simply refused to listen to what the anti-
communist had to say about communism. We had no reason

to trust what they said. 'Once foreign troops are withdrawn and we have gained our independence, we will listen to you', we thought. We did not realize that by then it would be too late.

We respected the anti-imperialist, anti-colonialist face of communism. That respect was a barrier against the claims of the anti-communists; it was a barrier that held firm even against the horror stories of the many refugees who fled communist regimes. It still holds firm in America today, where many people prefer to ignore the horror stories that the boat people tell, because to accept their stories would destroy a romantic idea of communist revolution. When I read Solzhenitsyn's *Gulag Archipelago*, I simply refused to believe it was true. I suspect that many people today have a similar difficulty in reading my book, *The Vietnam Gulag*.

With every defeat – first China in 1949, then North Vietnam in 1954, and finally South Vietnam in 1975 – the people of the West have seen themselves as incompetent at fighting communism. A good number of soldiers and diplomats, after fighting ineffectively for years and witnessing brutality after brutality, began to lose a sense of moral distinction between communism and democracy. Others clung to that distinction and exaggerated it into an apocalyptic battle between good and evil.

And in the same way that many of those involved failed to understand the situation, many who have looked back on Vietnam and other conflicts have failed to draw the right lessons. Some conservatives have wrongfully concluded that America lost in Vietnam because it was not brutal enough, because Americans could not bring themselves to lie and torture and assassinate as efficiently as the communists. Some have even thought that if we had only used the atomic bomb we would have won.

Likewise, some liberals have regretted that they did not support the right-wing anti-communist regime, now believing that they should have supported the lesser of two evils. Both of these groups fail to understand that the lesser evil *led* to the greater.

The South Vietnamese government also made serious mistakes. The hardline right-wing orientation of successive Saigon regimes often radicalized and alienated those who should have been made into allies. In many cases, the government's use of police brutality and similar tactics turned the loyal opposition into leftists, moderate leftists into reluctant communists, romantic Marxists into professional agents, and naive rebels into terrorists.

Hanoi and other communist regimes have taken effective advantage of these enormous strategic errors. Not only did they succeed in 'rallying all those who could be rallied', but they also caused dissension and conflict in the West simply by undertaking token reforms. This last was a particularly powerful tactic because it played into the Western desire to see reforms take place by themselves.

With each failure to defeat the communists, a desire to believe that they would reform anyway flared up in the West. Americans, in particular, are unused to admitting defeat, and sometimes seem to prefer to imagine that they have won.

With this background, those of us who would think seriously about communist reforms must be careful to distinguish genuine reforms from the reforms that we merely imagine and the token reforms that communists often undertake in order to distract their opponents. A quick example comes to mind: during the détente era, just two weeks after the Soviet announced their intention to withdraw 25 000 troops from East Germany, they began the invasion of Afghanistan. Shortly after that, Vietnamese communist troops invaded Cambodia, still denouncing American imperialism as loudly as possible.

As a former supporter of the Vietcong, I cannot claim always to have demonstrated good judgment in distinguishing hardline Stalinists from reform-minded communists. However, I can tell something about winning the hearts and minds of naive pro-communists like my younger self. My experiences have also given me a few ideas about how to push communist regimes in the direction of reform.

When I supported the Vietcong, I did so out of a misguided idealism. They claimed to stand for national independence – something that I strongly believed in. During the Vietnam War years, what did the anti-communists in Saigon and in the US stand for? What did they have to say that idealistic young men and women, that the Third-World people suffering under

colonial repression would care to hear? Anti-communism
alone is reactionary, it is a reaction against change, often
preached to people who are in desperate need of change. It
is associated with dictators and McCarthyite tactics.

It is impossible to overestimate the military value of these
feelings. In the jungles of Vietnam and in the Saigon prisons,
the Vietcong and other opposition forces truly believed that
they were fulfilling their commitment to peace and independence for their country. When a Vietcong soldier was killed
on the battlefield, his compatriots believed that he died for
his country. When a Vietcong killed an American, he truly
believed that he had killed an invader. Contrast that patriotic
fervor with the feelings of those defending the South. What
did ARVN or American soldiers believe as they fought and
died, as they killed their Vietnamese enemies? How many of
them felt that they were striking a blow for freedom?

It may seem simplistic, but the best way to wean the
naive young people and uneducated peasants of the Third
World away from Marxism is by offering a better alternative.
In the conflicts of the future, we will certainly fail if we
rely on right-wing regimes to fight against those who style
themselves as liberators. We will certainly fail if we simply
repeat the slogans of anti-communism. Unless we provide
spiritual nourishment to the people of the Third World,
unless we provide meaningful and concrete ideals that will
better the lives of those living under repressive governments,
unless we truly show a commitment to the values of individual
liberty, free institutions, representative governments, freedom
of speech and religion and freedom from oppression, the tide
of history will indeed be against us.

Fortunately, in the aftermath of Vietnam the United States
has become more careful in its support for anti-communist
regimes. This policy reflects a new understanding that, in the
long term, right-wing dictatorships fall into the hands of the
communists. It seems today that the US is learning from its
failure in Vietnam, while the communist camp is repeating
our earlier mistakes.

It is a cause for optimism that the Third World has begun
to look beneath what the Soviets say to see what they do. The
Soviets have lost credibility in Afghanistan and in Cambodia,
while the United States has gained it in the Philippines,

Panama, South Korea and elsewhere. Now we have another chance, a chance to challenge the Soviet Union for the hearts of a new generation of oppressed peoples and for the friendship of a host of young nations.

This challenge exerts a reformist pressure on how the Soviets treat the nations they control. People are beginning to see the Soviets, not the United States, supporting dictators and fighting liberation movements.

These events have important consequences. In some repressive right-wing countries, the liberation movements are not communist. And in a number of communist nations, the people are calling for reform – first in China, then Poland, and later the Soviet Union and Vietnam.

Reforms, particularly economic reforms, do seem to be taking place in these countries. Whether they succeed or fail will depend both on internal factors and on the West.

The ignorance and fanatical devotion to a cause that I found in the Vietnamese communist regime can be a very powerful force, particularly when there is a war to fight. But when peace came to Vietnam, the chief priority – apart from the internal power struggle – became economic. After the American withdrawal, the Hanoi regime proved a dismal failure at building a stable economy. Vietnam has recently followed the Soviet lead in admitting serious economic mistakes. When the threat they perceive from the West abates, communist countries are likely to turn their attention to economic matters.

Let us look more closely at some examples of communist reform. In China, Deng Xiaoping himself was a victim of the cultural revolution. Once he regained a leadership role, his eyes were open to the worst abuses of the communist system. If he had managed to remain in power throughout the early 1970s, I doubt that today's reforms, tentative as they are, would be taking place.

Vietnam has not experienced such a radical reform movement, in part because it has no leaders who were ever outside the system. Instead, a number of so-called pragmatic leaders are now replacing the more dogmatic generation who were Ho Chi Minh's contemporaries. One of the new leaders, Nguyen Van Linh, has been called Vietnam's 'Little Gorbachev'. But it remains to be seen whether he has the desire or the ability to bring real reform to Vietnam. One important sign is that

Hanoi has begun to take responsibility for its mistakes.

In the first few years after their victory, the Vietnamese communists blamed their problems on 'imperialist and expansionist foreigners and reactionaries'. Later, they blamed 'corruption, mismanagement and the right-wing spirit inside the party'. During the first years, the system's failures affected only the people, and the party did not care. Later, if affected party members. But only when the continuing series of economic failures began directly to affect party leaders did they begin to admit their mistakes.

Still, this admission was not an easy thing for Vietnam's party leadership. When Truong Chinh, Pham Van Dong, and Le Duc Tho resigned from the Politburo, their letter of resignation contained unprecedented confessions of mistakes and mismanagement. The party newspaper reported that the party and its top leaders had lost their reputation, their credibility and the loyalty of the Vietnamese people. This was not just a tactical apology. Only if the top leaders and the entire party accepted responsibility for these errors could the party and the regime be saved. In 1956, when a disastrous land reform program in the North killed thousands of people, only a few party leaders accepted personal responsibility. For the most senior leaders to accept responsibility for serious mistakes on the part of the whole party was unprecedented. Still, such acceptance of past mistakes reflects not so much an impulse toward capitalist democracy as toward self-preservation.

Such reforms have met with differing reactions in the West. Some conservatives have been overjoyed. Perhaps overestimating the rigidity of communist regimes, they see the merest bending as a sign of impending collapse. Others are more skeptical, denying that any substantive reforms have occurred. My sense is that these reforms are an opening that the West should take advantage of. Now is the time to push hard-line communist regimes in the direction of reform. Tactical and economic reforms create an opening toward substantive pro-Western developments. We do have the power to influence what happens.

Living in this country, it is easy to forget how powerful an idea democracy is. When we forget that, we lose sight of the tremendous advantages it has over the communist system. Let me list just a few:

– Democracies don't need to waste precious resources in policing their people or crushing dissent.

– The capitalist system affords the West such prosperity that it can provide for the needs of its people and at the same time ensure a sturdy defense; the Soviets must choose one or the other.

– People all over the world, even the most virulent anti-Americans, know that it is better to live in a democracy than in a communist country – the Soviets regulate the flow of people who want to leave. The American ideal attracts supporters from all over the world.

– Democracies have the flexibility to adapt to social and technological change while communist regimes are trapped by their fears and by the self-interest of their bureaucracies.

I offer these examples not as a definitive list, but merely to indicate some of our advantages in the battle against communism. However, even an overwhelming advantage cannot succeed by itself. We need to use what we have wisely. The most vigorous leaders of the communist world recognize that they face a nearly insurmountable problem. First in China, and now in the Soviet Union and in Vietnam, party leaders are trying to walk a delicate line between addressing the changing expectations of their people and keeping a firm hand on the reins of power. Their tightrope walk presents a crucial new challenge to the West. We can face that challenge by working for democracy wherever the opportunity presents itself. There is no single right line telling us what to do in all cases, but I believe that the following principles can help to guide us:

(1) In countries where a pro-communist war of liberation is already in full swing, we should not let the need to be decisive rush us into counterproductive actions. Remember that small countries value their independence and avoid unilateral policies. Be careful not to brand everyone in opposition to the government as communist. We should remember the communist strategy to 'rally all who can be rallied' and be wise enough to split the non-communist elements away from their deadly communist allies. Other-

wise, many in the center or on the left will fall into their hands.

(2) In anti-communist but repressive regimes, we should be careful to maintain contact with the opposition. Blindly supporting the government only encourages anti-American sentiment. We should work to address the needs of the people more effectively than the communists do.

(3) In communist countries where true popular liberation movements exist, we have to support them. *Support* them, not take them over. We should respect their right of self-determination and not impose our ideas on our allies. We should rely on the most effective forces rather than on those who obey us blindly. Once we decide to support them, we have to convince our people of the rightness of our cause. We must also be certain to develop a long-term strategy and stick to it. To assure a liberation movement of our support and suddenly withdraw that support is counterproductive and immoral.

(4) Finally, in communist countries where no armed opposition exists, we should not pay mercenaries to fight for our cause. We should support non-violent opposition movements, encourage more moderate communist leadership, and be ready to extend our friendship where appropriate.

To conclude, I believe that we should recognize our strengths and limitations, and use them to work effectively. We should neither minimize our strengths nor maximize our limitations. We fight communism to improve the lives of those living under it as well as to build a safer and more peaceful world for ourselves. Therefore we must fight not to kill communists or to harden their positions, but to change their minds about what makes a good society.

The day of communist revolutions is over. There are no more colonial powers controlling the Third World. It is time now for the West to take initiative and make a different kind of revolution — a revolution not *against* communism, but *for* democracy.

Part III
Unofficial Movements

13 Poland: Rebuilding Social Life
Jakub Karpinski

BACKGROUND: THE SYSTEM

According to official terminology, Poland is a socialist country (it belongs to the 'family of socialist countries'). This means in practice that the state tries to control everything, including the economy. In most domains – outside agriculture – the state is the only employer, which gives it considerable power to influence careers by firing, hiring and advancing people, often according to political criteria.

The state is ruled by the communist party, which is a mass organization of supporters of the authorities. In exchange for support, party members' careers are facilitated. Membership in the party is motivated by a desire for insurance against risk: there is a conviction that the system is stable and that security may be obtained when one joins its supporters. The party had more than three million members in 1979, but its membership declined in the early 1980s and in 1984 it was slightly more than two million.

The party-state has at its disposal the army, the police, the judiciary, the mass propaganda media and the state-controlled education system. This is true in all communist countries; what is specific to Poland is the widespread awareness of the negative implications of party-state control. A recurrent theme of the publications of the opposition and its activities is the problem of how to limit state omnipotence for the benefit of its citizens.

THE SOCIETY

We are now lucky to have at our disposal interesting and competent works by Polish sociologists. They give us an image of Polish society which is not very encouraging.

The economic and ecological situation in Poland is dramatic and is perceived as such by the Poles. About one-fifth of the nation lives below a very limited 'social minimum' standard, which means that they are on the verge of poverty.

Prospects for the young are particularly bad. The chances of getting a separate flat are almost non-existent. The social value of work is diminishing. Usually, work does not bring rewards. The youth wants to move outside the system, to family and private life, to private enterprise or abroad. People see prospects for the nation and for themselves as gloomy.

There is a strong perception of group differences, conflicts and injustices. The privileges stemming from connections with the power apparatus are considered to be particularly unjust. However, if differences in the standard of living reflect qualifications or education, they are generally accepted. Also – according to public opinion research – gains in the private sector are generally considered a legitimate reward for the risks involved.

For 30 years people in Poland have been asked by sociologists about the extent of their acceptance of the private sector of the economy. This acceptance grows. It is practically unanimous for agriculture, retail commerce, small services and crafts. About one-third of the population approves of unlimited freedom for private business in medium range industry, big commerce, and foreign trade. These, however, are social attitudes. Practice follows hesitantly, and state control prevails.

According to Polish sociologists, one-fourth of the population declares support for the authorities, for their political decisions, and the existing political system; one-fourth is openly against; one-half is in between, not interested, not involved, not decided. To declare opposition usually demands more courage than to declare support, therefore one can assume that declarations of opposition are often more serious and more central for the individual outlook than declarations of support.

The supporters of the authorities come not only from the power apparatus and party membership but also from the less educated and the less skilled strata. The opposition and its sympathizers – according to sociological research – are most numerous among the young and the better educated,

among non-party people and among the members of the intelligentsia and skilled workers.

SOLIDARITY UNDERGROUND

Created in the wake of strikes and agreements signed in
August 1980, Solidarity in 1980–81 combined many functions. It was a labor union, a social movement, a patriotic
organization – ten million strong, a type of movement without
precedence, perhaps not only in a communist country. In
December 1981, a well-designed and well-prepared military
and police operation, martial law – called in Polish *stan
wojenny* (the state of war) – had as its aim the destruction of
this union.

During the last six years the two principal sides of the
conflict, the communist authorities and the opposition, have
had opportunities to change their policies and to gather
experience.

Martial law ended legally in July 1983. Solidarity had then
a territorial organization, a clandestine leadership composed
of known former leaders, and a charismatic chairman – Lech
Walesa. Today Solidarity still has a central leadership, but it
seems to be even less formal, with a more diverse network of
groups than during martial law.

Martial law created the contemporary underground in
Poland. At this point an explanation may be useful:
underground does not necessarily refer to people in hiding.
During martial law, some well-known Solidarity leaders were
in hiding, forming an underground leadership of the union.
Now activists are underground only part-time (with very few
exceptions). If, for instance, people print books underground,
without the state's permission, both books and printers soon
emerge above ground.

Under martial law, some of the underground's aims were in
a sense conservative. Many people in the opposition wanted
to come back to the situation that existed before December
1981, by restoring Solidarity's legal status as an organization
empowered to negotiate with the authorities.

But past experience with 'normal' communism suggests
that the legal existence of Solidarity was an anomaly. This

anomaly, however, constituted for the underground the main point of reference. It was paradise lost. In thinking about how to regain this paradise, people wanted to use methods which, they thought, had proved effective.

It is known that mass movements are inspired by images from the past. Today, Poland is greatly influenced by a certain image, that of August 1980, when a general strike followed by negotiations ended in an agreement with the authorities, who granted concessions that imposed limits on state control.

The image was colorful, and what happened in August 1980 had very important consequences. Fourteen months of legal Solidarity gave people in Poland a taste of freedom, democracy, trust and independence; it gave meaning to people's lives. All of this was rather uncommon under 'normally' developed communism.

Another historical image, however, interplays with the former one: that of martial law. This recalls not only beatings, killings and arrests, but also the ability of the rulers to crush the opposition. One can envisage a general strike as an effective measure only if the authorities renounce violence (during martial law striking plants were attacked by combined police and military detachments).

At the very beginning of martial law, a controversy emerged in the opposition between followers of the general strike scheme and others who defended a less spectacular idea which nevertheless proved to be fruitful: the idea of long preparations in which step by step the society would become organized independently on the party-state, even if initially it would be through small, rather informal networks of individuals producing clandestine newspapers or monitoring work conditions or human rights abuses. In this way, the elements of civil society were to be recreated.

These preparations for a civil society have been in a sense in conflict with the pre-martial law Solidarity patterns of operation. There were two axes of difference: *centralization-decentralization and union-non-union activities*.

Solidarity in 1980–81 was successful through centralization, owing to a unified leadership able to negotiate. The new underground was to be decentralized. One of the advantages of this solution was that the police have more trouble destroying what is decentralized.

But this solution was also a source of tension. It was not easy for some Solidarity leaders to relinquish a unified, centralized way of operation, and Solidarity authorities in hiding often tried to control the emerging independent groupings and their different activities.

As for the second difference, as a legally recognized labor union, Solidarity focused its interests on the problems of wages, prices and work conditions, which had to be negotiated with the state as the main, nearly monopolistic employer and owner of the national economy, which determined the prices of most goods. As an underground, newly independent organization, Solidarity could no longer conduct negotiations, and the main activities and interests shifted from typical labor union issues to publishing, developing and spreading culture, and education. Various underground groups concentrated on monitoring specific fields: human rights, health care, national economy, ecology and housing. What we have witnessed is a functional differentiation of the oppositional, partially underground, activities.

What Solidarity was and was not was roughly clear until December 1981. People tended to subsume every possible kind of opposition under the union's protection and under the union's name. Nowadays, this is no longer the case. The criteria for Solidarity membership are mostly psychological, although there are thousands of activists. On the national level, Solidarity is a reserve army difficult to count and mobilize.

As long as Solidarity is not officially recognized, it will have no legal right to negotiate, and that decisively hampers its labor union activities. Solidarity cannot accept the rules of the system, such as the principle of the leading role of the party apparatus, but it also does not wish to remain outside the system without recognition as a legitimate negotiating partner.

The authorities press Solidarity leaders to declare that they want to be part of the system, despite all bitter experiences with communist power. According to some militants, conciliatory declarations only create confusion and are counterproductive. The union leaders try to find a balance between conciliatory signals to the government and signals of strength to union activists and supporters.

Sending such mixed signals is a necessary political game
with practical results. In August 1987 Lech Walesa refused
to accept $1 million donated by the US Congress to the
union. He suggested that the money be used instead for
health care. His move was criticized by practically-minded
activists, who believed that the needs of the union should
have taken precedence over a philanthropic action intended,
in their view, to regain respectability for the union in the eyes
of the authorities.

OPPOSITION AT LARGE

Now Solidarity has allies and competitors both above ground
and underground. Active opposition in Poland includes more
than Solidarity alone. Solidarity is mostly active at the factory
level, monitoring work conditions and denouncing abuses
of the employees' rights. Such activities are only slightly
coordinated on the regional level; at the national level it
produces statements from time to time, but since 1982 it
has been so decentralized that it has been difficult for it to
call successfully for a national strike.

The most popular opposition activity is to publish, distribute and read books and journals that have circumvented
state censorship. Printers and editors are very careful not
to lose their independence, which also means independence
from Solidarity authorities. The same is true about human
rights monitoring groups or the independent network called
OKNO, which deals with education, culture, higher learning
and health care problems.

Even more independent of Solidarity are political organizations, the best organized of them being Fighting Solidarity.
These organizations usually stress the need for Poland's
national independence. They proclaim their support for the
opposition in other communist countries, publish texts about
other nations under communism and texts in the languages of
neighboring nations, mainly Czech, Ukrainian and Russian.
Some Solidarity leaders and advisors avoid such concerns and
activities, considering them obstacles to winning recognition
from the authorities. Fighting Solidarity, like other political
organizations, fights mostly by publishing periodicals, many

of them appearing in the Lower Silesia (Wroclaw) region, the organization's stronghold.

One can distinguish concentric circles of involvement in the opposition. The largest one is to behave legally but not according to the authorities' expectations, such as boycotting the elections (30–40 per cent of the population in 1984 and 1985 and during the 1987 referendum, a situation unusual under communist rule). The readership of the underground press is more limited (sociologists estimate it at one million). The most active involvement is to participate in one of the underground groups, called *structure*. This word, borrowed from scientific terminology, has become very popular since the imposition of martial law. Structures are networks, groups or organizations, which until 1986 (the year of the recent amnesty) usually have not disclosed their membership publicly. They may use the name of Solidarity, and may be loosely connected with local and national Solidarity governing and coordinating commissions, though this is not always so. Structures rally around underground publications, which gives them additional social importance. Sometimes structures are alliances between independent union and non-union groups and organizations.

These groups adopt issues, express their ideas and try to influence the outside world, including Solidarity governing bodies. Detailed texts and lively disputes concern the future of Poland. People discuss legal problems, such as the future constitution of the country, its economy and foreign policy. Socialists quarrel with liberals, who advocate free markets and limits on state control. Writers in underground publications argue about alliances of the future Poland: whether they should be with the future Ukraine or with the future Russia. To an observer, these discussions may appear abstract, but their importance is that the dreams and hopes of the political opposition are located outside the existing political system.

The recent milder and more tolerant policies in the Soviet Union have been welcomed in Poland, and it is generally that the more civilized the Soviet system is and the more enlightened are its citizens, the better it is for Poland. But approval does not imply a wish to imitate. Gorbachev's reforms started from a very low level of individual freedom and state tolerance, and therefore if they were imitated in Poland on the same level, it would not be an improvement, but a step back.

The idea of *glasnost*, to take an example, does not seem to be very persuasive in Poland, because – due to the underground – accurate information is already available there. This includes information on the economy, the ecological situation and those events in recent history that have been expunged from official textbooks.

Some internal communist problems are also generally not very attractive, like the idea, timidly touched upon in the Soviet Union and so popular in the West, of rehabilitating Trotsky and other Bolshevik leaders. Many of them, officially forgotten, were certainly important in the history of the communist movement, but from a Polish perspective there is hardly a reason to rehabilitate Trotsky, just as there is hardly a reason to rehabilitate Lenin. People know that both of them guided the Soviet military offensive against Poland during the Polish-Soviet war in 1920, and both of them, together with other Soviet leaders, created a system which they and their heirs finally succeeded in exporting to Poland.

Instead of the *glasnost* propounded by the authorities, during the past ten years underground publishing has been the most significant development. Every year, hundreds of titles are published clandestinely, without being subjected to state censorship. There are also hundreds of independent journals, from one-page weekly news bulletins to thick literary and political quarterlies.

Underground publishing is an oxygen for Polish culture. It is valuable in itself, for it provides information, distributes the statements of independent groups and gives novelists and historians an opportunity to publish without state control. This method of publishing also has an interesting side-effect: underground competition inclines the authorities to decrease censorship. For instance, some important works of Polish émigré writers (like Milosz and Gombrowicz) were initially published abroad, later republished underground, and finally re-edited above ground by state publishing houses, with the permission of the censors.

Another side-effect of underground publishing is its function as a school of enterprise and organization. Bigger publishing houses publish around 15 titles a year, each title in at least one thousand copies. The managers must have entrepreneurial skills: they must know how to invest, how to find capital and large quantities of raw materials, machines, staff and space. The main publishers have created a clandestine foundation which gives loans and grants and acts as an insurance company in case of police confiscation of printing equipment or large quantities of books.

THE CATHOLIC CHURCH

In communist countries, the Catholic Church is often persecuted, and in some cases subordinated or banned altogether. In contemporary Poland the Catholic Church is stronger than in many non-communist countries, and, interestingly, since martial law, it has assumed some functions which legal Solidarity fulfilled previously.

Just as in 1981 Solidarity protected independent journalism, publishing and social research, the Church now plays the role of universal shield – in quite earthly matters, from culture to agriculture. The Church organizes pastoral activities for professional groups, helping them to understand their situation and the ethical problems they encounter. Christian Culture Weeks are organized in churches throughout the country, with the participation of the best artists, actors, historians and literary critics. Journalists come from newspapers from the official party press to the catholic press. The church now plans to establish an Agricultural Foundation to aid private farmers. These plans recently took the form of an Agricultural Church Committee, which intends to provide machine equipment for the farmers and to finance a program improving the water supply in the countryside.

The Catholic Church emerged from martial law stronger than before. The authorities probably did not wish to fight simultaneously on too many fronts. Building new churches requires the authorities' permission, which until the 1980s was not usually granted. At present, many new churches are being built throughout the country. Dioceses and religious orders got permission for new or renewed weekly or monthly periodicals. The Church has not ceased to be a source of values and an alternative information network. It is a moral authority and an independent educator.

The Church rituals – the sacraments, pilgrimages, Papal visits – are widely accessible, and those who participate are not punished. The Church thus attracts many, while people active in the opposition are a minority of primarily the younger and better-educated large factory workers and big-city dwellers. Practicing Solidarity rituals such as strikes, marches or even badge-wearing often provokes repression. American Vice-President George Bush behaved according to the customs of the land when, on his visit to Father Popieluszko's grave, he displayed a Solidarity banner which had been hidden in his pocket.

According to public opinion research, the period of the legal existence of Solidarity (1980–81) was the most positive one in postwar history. Solidarity Chairman Lech Walesa ranks high on the scale of prestige and confidence, though not higher than John Paul II or the Polish primate, Josef Glemp.

INDEPENDENT ABOVE GROUND ACTIVITIES

The Catholic Church is not the only institution which gives shelter to the opposition and which has helped some underground activities to emerge above ground (mainly in the field of publishing and culture). There are links between the opposition and official institutions, because institutions are official only to a certain degree.

Institutions often leave room for independence, and some serve as a cover for opposition activities, supporting or complementing them. Despite tough laws on higher education adopted in July 1985, the best universities still enjoy a degree of autonomy, and the authorities still have difficulties with elected self-governing bodies in the learning institutions and in the universities.

The situation of the Polish economy is dramatic, not only on the macroeconomic but also on the household level. The drama is clearly felt during everyday shopping. The authorities announce one price increase after another, but they proclaim also that in some areas they are ready to tolerate more private enterprise. This way they repeat 1944 promises made by the communist government created for Poland in Moscow (called the Polish Committee of National Liberation).

It is true that after 1944 some private economic activity has been possible, but it has always been difficult and endangered. Private agriculture has prevailed, and – on a limited scale – there has existed private commerce and craft. In the 1980s new possibilities have emerged for small industry and services. For instance, former journalists and assistant professors established an independent cooperative advising how to build private homes. They publish an officially permitted monthly, *Murator*, which gives legal and technical advice to prospective builders.

Another example of above ground but independent activity is the Cracow Industrial Society, which deals with the problems of private enterprises and has finally received official permission to exist (a similar association still awaits registration in Warsaw). The authorities seem now to tolerate entrepreneurs and to grant them some organizational possibilities. However, the state is less apt to make concessions to its own employees. Their rights to have independent labor organizations are not recognized, despite Poland's ratification of the Conventions of the International Labor Organization. The rights of entrepreneurs have thus taken precedence over the rights of employees.

CONCLUSIONS

Possibilities for above ground activity have recently expanded in those areas that are not usually associated with the communist vision of the ideal society. In Poland, much can be done under the aegis of the Church, through its networks of publications and organizations; other possibilities have emerged in the private sector of the economy, although not yet in the officially-recognized labor unions.

The state is the guardian of official institutions, and it is not inclined to share its power. The state's efforts to dominate such institutions have been only partially successful however. Even less successful have been the state's efforts to dominate minds and souls, to rule over information, education and social values. Contemporary Polish culture is largely independent of the authorities – a situation which, again, is not typical in communist countries.

Although any single achievement of the independent movements in Poland is fragile, taken together these achievements cannot be easily destroyed. Their force stems from, among other sources, their decentralization and fragmentation. What is underground and what is above ground, especially the Catholic Church and some official institutions, are not separate worlds. Due to them, a *civil society* is now being rebuilt. It has its own authorities, social rules and norms, entrepreneurs, experts and negotiators. It formulates ideas, creates independent culture and expresses various opinions. It has its literature, history, data banks and, most important, its organizations, which the authorities often consider illegal. The authorities have persecuted their members with varying intensity (during martial law strongly, later, with greater leniency).

Creating independent organizations and institutions is not an easy task. It goes against the principles of Leninist social organization, according to which only such organizations which can be controlled by the avant garde communist party and which the party can use as 'transmission belts' are permitted. The legal recognition of Solidarity, as an organization not controlled by the party, encounters strong resistance from authorities who, nevertheless, tolerate some 'liberal' changes: they permit – with hesitation – small-scale private commerce and services, a few real cooperatives and independent associations, and the Catholic Church's religious, social and cultural activities.

Future changes in Poland will depend on the interplay of several factors. One is the will of Poles to build an independent social life despite obstacles; this will has proved to be strong. A second factor is the tolerance of the authorities, depending on their perception of what constitutes a threat to their power and to the system they wish to preserve. A third factor is Soviet tolerance of changes in Poland. Finally, independent social forces in other countries within the Soviet sphere reinforce one another: the total is greater than the sum of its parts. The Soviets would have difficulty suppressing simultaneous pressure in several countries, and if, at a given moment, they do not want to antagonize Western opinion by military intervention, such changes, although not approved, may be tolerated.

Whatever the external conditions and the willingness of the authorities to tolerate independence, what has already been built in Poland constitutes a firm foundation for changes toward the basic goals of the opposition: the establishment of a self-governing, independent and pluralistic society, a more rational economy, and more individual freedom and democracy.

14 The Emerging Civil Society

Zagorka Golubovic

'. . . A society has begun to emerge from under the shroud of an all-encompassing state.' (Robert C. Tucker)
'Our hope grapples with our despair. . . The changes are as unavoidable as they are risky. . .' (Adam Michnik)

I want to discuss the statement that 'real socialist' systems are incapable of producing self-correcting mechanisms, that is, of reforming themselves from within. The advocates of this statement argue that resistance to reforms is built into the nature of a totalitarian system with a power monopoly based on a mono-organizational bureaucracy. Others who are less resolute in denying the possibilities of reforms of existing socialist states often restrict their prognoses to economic reforms alone. Failing to learn the lessons of history, they avoid the question of whether economic reforms have a real chance in a system in which politics dominates the sub-systems.

My conviction concerning the potential for reform in Eastern Europe, and the USSR as well, is not grounded upon an optimistic estimation of the good will of Gorbachev, nor upon hope for more radical reformist projects originating from above. My estimation is based upon evidence inferred from a complex approach to the social dynamics of these societies. If we consider only the dominant social forces which are officially recognized as the sole legitimate sources of social change, we lose sight of a much richer potential. That is why we should consider initiatives for social change which come from below, being usually beyond the boundaries of the officially recognized forces, as well as within-system initiatives.

A second point which I want to highlight concerns the question of how reforms can be implemented, that is, is a gradual, peaceful evolution of actually existing socialism possible?[1] In order to answer these questions, the possibility of changing the principal traits of these systems should be re-examined. First and foremost among these is the party's leading role, which implies the exclusion of political pluralism and an independent public opinion, as well as what this role implies, that there is a sole officially recognized arbiter which imposes political/ideological criteria over all dimensions of social life. The result of this has been a predominance of state/political power and, consequently, the disappearance of civil society.

A study of the possibilities of reforming these societies should thus include the following: first, a reassessment of the assumed characteristics of the existing socialist states in order to find out whether they have remained unchanged or whether historical experience has given evidence of their changeability (including the 1956 Hungarian revolution, the 1956–81 movements in Poland, the 1968 reforms in Czechoslovakia and the Yugoslav experience); second, it should answer the question, to what extent can these systems embark on significant changes without provoking a threat of the bloc's intervention (when Eastern Europe is concerned) or an expansion of the conservative or even neo-Stalinist forces (when the USSR is in question).

It is beyond any doubt that these societies badly need reforms, from both a practical viewpoint, to solve the problem of the system's dysfunctionality and avoid further decay, and from an ideological imperative, to provide a new legitimation for the power élite's claim to be the true guardian of 'real socialism'. However, the ruling élite's awareness that reforms are necessary is mixed with their fears of consequences which may undermine their dominant, privileged position. Two opposing forces are thus in action: motivation for reforms and a strong resistance to them.

The true dilemma is thus not whether these societies can be reformed, because some reforms are inevitable, but rather *what kind* of reforms are possible. The issue is what can be changed and what cannot, within the context of a predominantly political and mono-organization institutional order.

Here we have to clarify the concept of reform. When examining the possibilities of reforming the socialist states, does one imply *a within-system* change which alters existing institutions or a break through the existing order which gives room for the introduction of new institutions and communications? Is only the former related to reforms while the latter necessarily requires revolutions? Or can reform occur on two levels, one within the existing institutions and another which transcends the institutional order, as new forms of organization and communication become parts of an evolving social structure?

I want to clarify my position by defining reform in the latter terms. I shall thus consider present-day prospects for reforms not only in their actual form as initiated by Gorbachev, but also through a broader historical perspective. When examining historical experiences, we note a variety of grass-roots-level changes in different socialist states that are worthy of being studied. A twofold direction for reforms thus emerges, so that we can reasonably doubt the statement which declares 'reforms from above' as the only possible way of reforming existing socialist states. Historical experience has proven both routes to reform to be possible and legitimate, despite the resistance of the ruling élite to social change in general, and to those changes initiated from below in particular. Moreover, it is the latter which may become most promising when an independent society awakens and begins to play a role that no longer be ignored because of the society's increased capacity for survival.

That certain reforms will necessarily be undertaken in Soviet-type societies is beyond doubt. But how far can reforms penetrate the systemic boundaries which characterize an authoritarian regime? Can they affect the principle of the party's leading role, which has been inviolable thus far? A debate goes on as to whether democratization or merely a liberalization will be possible under the circumstances. However, when the experiences of liberalization are taken into consideration, in Yugoslavia for example, they have shown the following: even a limited liberalization of the economy does not involve a mere loosening of central control and shop-floor level reorganizations; it demands, at least to a certain degree, the revamping of the power structure which blocks the development of enterprise autonomy, which is a precondition for a free market economy. It thus challenges the basis upon which the political bureaucracy (the nomenklatura system) rests. Otherwise, economic reforms inevitably fail. Similarly, a more liberal attitude towards private initiatives does not affect economic enterprises alone, for such activities may penetrate into various aspects of society from economy to culture.

In order to expand these regimes' capacities for evolution, reform is needed like air, as Gorbachev puts it. Reform is, in fact, a question of the power élites' survival, because they are at present confronted with certain unsurmountable obstacles to further development. Their 'inviolable principles' have become the strongest barriers to resolving the crisis. The principles of monolithism and centralized management suppress initiative and creativity to produce a diffused bureaucratic parasitism and sterility. If a reconstruction that may revive evolutionary potential fails to take place in the existing socialist states, the continuation of these practices will discredit the ideologies and blueprints which proclaim commitment to building socialism while they actually destroy the possibilities of evolution.

As to the scope of reforms, the limited institutional opportunities within the existing structure do not allow spectacular changes, but rather step-by-step alterations. However, even within such a restricted framework, that is, room for some needed reforms, partially thanks to changing official views on management and worker and citizen participation. This is what Michnik points to when speaking of the possibility of limited reforms from above (a 'counter-reformation', as he calls it) to open the way toward new attitudes about the philosophy of political comprises.[2]

A test of reforms which may penetrate beyond the surface of established behaviour may be made as follows: first, in as much as the existence of a *variety of interests* is recognized, a necessity of creating mechanisms which would enable society to deal with its contradictions and conflicts is indicated as a next step. This also implies that a dogmatic assumption of a non-conflictual 'monolithic social interest' is abandoned. When different interests are recognized and given legal status, the conflict of interests must be introduced as a concept demanding institutional regulation, which can no longer be a prerogative of the state alone, since the state loses its status as the only 'entrepreneur' and representative of all social interests.

The Yugoslav case is indicative as a half-way solution represented by the late party ideologue Edvard Kardelj's theory of the 'pluralism of self-governing interests'. An ambivalent attitude appears in that various economic interests are acknowledged while political differences are denied. In other words, a recognition of plurality of interests is not followed by the legal recognition of pluralism in the forms of their expressions.

Second, when a 'monolithic ideology' is supposed to constitute the foundation of a system, the emergence of parallel or 'alternate forms' of communication in culture and other fields is a reliable indication of favorable conditions for social change. Such 'alternative communications' have already won the right to exist in Poland, Hungary, Yugoslavia and even Bulgaria, despite more or less frequently applied measures of 'selective repression'. As a more complex culture which is no longer easily controllable evolves, more space is created for a variety of relatively independent activities, which may be a reliable sign of the emergence of a 'civil society' gradually liberating itself from the domination of the political apparatus. Although there is only a limited chance that civil society may be institutionalized within Soviet-type systems, it arises spontaneously and cannot be fully suppressed by political means.

However, the necessary moves will not be attained solely through initiatives from above, although it is there that the movement has always begun, and to a certain degree will continue to do in these societies. It is therefore more realistic to predict that a plurality of ideas and communications may enter through the 'back doors', gradually earning the right to exist through continuous pressures from below.

It is important to determine which needs and interests for social change, if any, coincide for both political élites and independent social groups interested in new forms of participation and conduct. The political élites' interest in reforms is a matter of necessity: it is neither a personal wish nor a liberal attitude on the part of leading figures. It stems from their need to reaffirm the legitimacy that has been so profoundly shaken under Stalin and during the period of Brezhnev's neo-Stalinist policies. For this reason, it seems to me, too much attention has been paid to Gorbachev's personality traits, while what is lacking is a profound analysis of the causes generating the need for social change. The problem is whether the need for new legitimacy, stimulated from above, can be reconciled with the population's need for greater autonomy. If more freedom of initiative and relative independence for social groups occurs without threatening to destroy the system, this might bring about the mutual satisfaction of needs to enable the necessary reforms. Certain indications of this sort are already visible in terms of a growing sensibility on both sides concerning the need for reform.[3] For example, Andrei Sakharov took a positive attitude to Gorbachev's reforms; certain moves within 'Solidarity' indicate the formulation of a program for reforms. At the same time, we see Gorbachev's more flexible stand concerning alternate opinions and 'political delicts'. (It may seem paradoxical that the Yugoslav authorities follow a more dogmatic policy in regards to 'verbal delicts', irrespective of the numerous public demands for the abolition of that article from the Criminal Code.)

Liberalization generated the unintended changes associated with the Yugoslav developments of the sixties, which resulted in the retrograde steps undertaken by the leadership in the seventies, which reinforced political domination and even re-Stalinization. It is hence understandable why a shift from liberalization to a tightening of control continues in these societies. Increased autonomy of the society's components decreases the political apparatus' capacity for control. This may seem too dangerous to a bureaucratic mind, to which a firm-hand policy is more acceptable as a means of defending 'order' against 'anarchistic disorder'. Such fears may affect the political élites' attitudes to the pressures from below, leading them to interpret them as threats to the system's legitimacy.

Nevertheless, one should be aware of the changing climate, not only thanks to Gorbachev's 'revolution from above', but also as a result of the continuous resistance to official policies in Poland, Hungary and Yugoslavia. The new climate in the USSR manifests itself in changes hardly imaginable some time ago, as Zdenek Mlynař emphasizes,[4] such as Gorbachev's recognition that past practices have not been successful and led to crisis, and that changes in management are necessary; or the current tolerance for raising previously forbidden questions and seeking alternative solutions, including consideration of the concept of self-management.

When certain authors estimate these changes as modest and unlikely to overstep the remaining principles of the system,[5] they disregard the fact these are necessary pre-conditions for concessions which may create opportunities for further evolution. The case of Poland is indicative: steps taken from 1956 to 1981 by the opposition have challenged official policy and led to new concessions enlarging the scope for independent action, regardless of the futility of hoping for more spectacular changes. The Yugoslav experience shows that the idea of self-government has deeply penetrated the minds of Yugoslav citizens. It is now treated as almost a 'natural right' which workers call upon when it is violated by bureaucratic powers. This is one of the reasons for the frequent strikes in Yugoslavia today, which have taken a political character rather than a purely economic one. This view of self-government has been adopted despite shortcomings in both its conception and practice, and despite the fact that its institutional forms have often been used as a means of manipulation.

A current development is the emergence of various forms of 'immature' political pluralism and the change of the so far dominant cultural pattern of public conformism.[6] Another factor is the lessening of the authoritarian regimes' capacities to control the budding non-institutional forms of conduct and culture and their greater ability to learn and respond to the problems, even if only on a pragmatic basis.[7] These elements provide the empirical grounds upon which analyses should rely when estimating the self-reforming potential of these societies.

The developments underlying the potential for significant social change in existing socialist states may be briefly summed up as follows: first, breaks from the monolithic structure of social control and conduct have already generated more complex 'parallel structures'. A strictly mono-organizational type of society no longer exists in Eastern Europe, while decentralization of management in Yugoslavia has gone far beyond ideology which implies a one-party monopoly. In Eastern Europe, this may not be recognizable at the institutional level, but even there the range of social conduct cannot be understood in terms of institutionalized forms alone.

Second, a dogmatic economic theory has also been broken by the introduction of differentiated forms of ownership. With the recognition of the market and commodity production, a mixed economy is now developing within the 'socialist' community. This may lay the grounds for greater autonomy of enterprises, and for enhanced participation in the decision-making process by the producers.

Third, a 'civil society' – even though immature and unique – is gaining its right to exist, despite the refusal of the ruling élite to accept the idea of a society independent of the state. The seeds of a modern democratic society have been planted in a 'socialist land' in which dissent has nowadays become a real part of the social scene. Living with dissent as a permanent expression of society's conflicting nature suggests a necessity to learn to compromise in order to meet newly arising needs and interests and avert open social conflicts.

Fourth, the emergence of a critical and increasingly independent public opinion, with a new role for the press (on fairly legal grounds in Yugoslavia, in semi-legal and underground forms in Poland), is a phenomenon that the authorities have to deal with. It is a first step toward the conceptualization and materialization of reforms.

Last but not least, since ideology has been reduced to a mere ritual, greater flexibility and openness of mind, the coexistence of a variety of ideas and beliefs and a more diffuse cultural scene have become possible. This situation allows a greater possibility for the unfettered existence of more differentiated forms of officially unrecognized communication. In the political sphere, the authorities recognize that they can no longer count on the unswerving loyalty of their mentally emancipated citizens.[8]

This by no means implies that the system of one-party rule has been cast off, or that the domination of the Marxist-Leninist ideology has been rejected, although it is being questioned. Introducing 'alien' elements into a previously unbroken monopoly of power and ideology has shaken the system, and the powerholders have failed to reaffirm all-embracing control over social life. A readjustment of policies is badly needed, as shown by the growing emphasis on the primacy of political changes. This new approach – almost unanimously shared by Yugoslav public opinion and increasingly popular in Hungary – challenges the traditional view that economic change alone can solve systemic dysfunctions. In conclusion, we should see Eastern Europe in its complex dynamics instead of sticking to a preconceived model. It is necessary to discard a schematic view limited to the dominant institutionalized social forces and corresponding confrontations, which loses sight of the immense variety of social, political and cultural processes whose interplay has brought about 'alternative forms' and new confrontations.

NOTES

1. Adam Michnik, 'Gorbachev, glasnost and perestroika: Policy views', *East European Reporter*, vol. 2, No. 3, 1987, p. 34.
2. Adam Michnik, ibid., p. 34.
3. For information see 'Tygodnik Mazowsze', No. 207, April 1987, published in English in *Uncensored Poland New Bulletin*, London, 29 May 1987, pp. 26–39, under the title 'Solidarity's position on the situation in the Polish economy and the directions for reconstruction'.
4. Zdenek Mlynař, 'The Chances of Gorbachev's Reforms', paper prepared for the Belgrade's conference on 'Possibilities of Reforms in the Socialist States', pp. 1–2. (The conference – organized by the Centre for Philosophy and Social Theory at the Institute of Social Sciences, University of Belgrade – was scheduled to be held in July 1987 but prohibited by the authorities.)
5. See Vladimir Tismaneanu, 'Neo-Stalinism and Reform Communism', *Orbis*, Summer 1986, pp. 270–1. All the changes such as: 'loosening of censorship' and 'a less patronizing attitude toward the intelligentsia', as well as 'limitations on the KGB' and 'a new approach to the issues of legality and human rights' – are treated by the author as not being 'a dramatic reconsideration of the dogmatic underpinnings of the Soviet system', p. 270. The above listed changes may not seem so 'dramatic' seen from without, but for those who have lived under the so far prevailing conditions of these regimes, they have a great significance because they have brought a wave of more relaxed conduct, promising the possibility of a new way of life as well, provided that changes continue in the same direction.
6. Robert C. Tucker, *Political Culture and Leadership in Soviet Russia, From Lenin to Gorbachev*; W.W. Norton, New York, 1987, pp. 184–5.
7. Moshe Lewin, *Foreword* to Basil Kerblay's *Modern Soviet Society*, Methuen, London, 1983, p. XXII.

8. For a more detailed description and a theoretical conceptualization of the Yugoslav developments, see my analysis, 'Yugoslav society and "real socialism", The present-day crisis of the Yugoslav system and the possibilities of evolution', in Zagorka Golubovic and Svetozar Stojanovic, *The Crisis of the Yugoslav System*, Study No. 14 of the series 'Crisis in Soviet-Type Systems', directed by Zdenek Mlynař and a Scientific Council, Munich, 1986.

15 Charter 77 and Other Independent Movements
Jan Kavan

Several months ago I read a long article in the *New York Times* on Czechoslovakia. It painted a picture of a contented population which has accepted the status quo and enjoys its cars, TV sets and country cottages. The only discordant voice among this seemingly satisfied mass of consumerism was that of the dissidents in Charter 77. [As events have evolved in Czechoslovakia, and the revolution swept away the communist regime, the Charter became the backbone of Civic Forum, the country's most popular political force. Therefore, this essay has enduring historical significance. (Eds)]

To some extent, the picture of the silent consumer is correct. There is a crippling demoralization caused by the two capitulations that have occurred within a single generation. In 1938 the Czechoslovak government capitulated under pressure from its Western allies, and the country was occupied without resistance. Thirty years later, the Czechoslovak government, led by Alexander Dubcek, capitulated under pressure from its Eastern allies, led by the Red Army, and the country was once again occupied without resistance. The result has been widespread apathy, skepticism and bitterness; the prevailing atmosphere of conformism influences even people for whom the latest defeat is just history. The silence, is however, that of a silenced majority and is the silence of disagreement. The Chartists appear to be a tiny minority only because, unlike so many others, they have found the courage to challenge the prevailing apathy and to defy the government's rule by fear. They frequently express aloud what the silenced majority actually thinks.

Guile and conformist behavior allow people to avoid danger, and some even survive in relative comfort. Consumer-oriented people everywhere are reluctant to sacrifice material gains for moral integrity. The regime is no longer totalitarian in the sense described by Western scholars in the 1950s, but it there is still a system of absolute state control over all areas of human life. As the sole employer and owner of all the means of production, the regime finds it relatively easy to manipulate individuals and it no longer has to resort to mass terror. It can, however, function smoothly only by extinguishing civil society in its entirety. All genuinely independent activities threaten the entire system, which defends itself by imprisoning for 'subversion of the republic' activists who refuse to be intimidated and to conform.

However, I do not want to dwell on the gloomy conditions in the Soviet bloc or to add to the publicity for Gorbachev's attempts to make them more palatable and to strengthen the system responsible for them. I merely wish to highlight what I consider one of the most important developments of the past decades – the nascent cooperation between the independent movements in several Soviet bloc countries, especially Poland, Czechoslovakia, Hungary and East Germany.

I choose as my starting point Charter 77's international contacts, for the following reasons: (1) Charter 77 is a good example of an independent group whose importance, because of the conditions in Czechoslovakia mentioned above, cannot be evaluated in numerical terms and whose supporters are convinced of the need to internationalize their struggle, some of them having risked imprisonment for it; (2) Charter 77 is the oldest human rights movement in the area and has the longest history of international contacts; (3) Charter 77 is politically quite heterogenous and thus has to put forward positions acceptable to a variety of its constituent groups, a capacity that is particularly valuable when faced with the diversity of interests within Eastern Europe; (4) Charter 77's consistent, seven-year long dialogue with the Western peace movement (and some of the internal discussion the dialogue provoked) has enabled its leading activists to formulate a theoretical framework which has proved useful even in exchanges among East Europeans.

CHARTER 77 AS AN ICE-BREAKER

Simply by calling things by their own names, rejecting the 'as if' game played throughout the Soviet bloc and 'accepting only the authority of truth' (Havel), Charter 77 was able to expose the hypocrisy of the system and challenge its very legitimacy. The work of Charter 77 has also created a fertile atmosphere for the emergence and development of other independent groups, by helping to discover the limits of what can be done and by drawing most of the authorities' fire onto itself. These groups include the cultural underground, music groups outside the underground's sphere, the parallel university (also known as Patočka university or the unofficial seminars), samizdat publishing, independent ecological groups, Living Room Theater, unofficial exhibitions of nonconformist painters and sculptors and so on. Some of them have flourished nearby Charter's umbrella, or were outside it. Others were directly underneath it and thus exposed to greater persecution; this was the case, for example, for the Committee for the Defense of the Unjustly Prosecuted (VONS).

In times of crisis, the importance of such groups far exceeds their numerical strength; only in calmer and more normal societies is mass participation such an important factor. Vaclav Havel observed that 'Charter 77 has a sort of electrifying effect which charges its surrounding and in turn becomes a political factor. It manages to influence the entire sphere of social consciousness which, normally speaking, is prey to manipulation by the regime'. This is perhaps a slight exaggeration, but Havel encapsulated the situation perfectly when he colorfully described the Charter as 'an ice-breaker with a kamikaze crew'.

INTERNATIONALIZATION OF CIVIL MOVEMENTS

Jiři Dienstbier, a well known journalist in the 1960s, a former Charter 77 spokesperson and a political prisoner, said once that 'Charter 77 has proved to be. . . a germ of civil society'. This point is crucial. Charter is not left or right, it is not pro-Reagan or pro-Gorbachev. Its supporters, politically very heterogeneous, are united by their determination to work for the renewal and further development of a civil society. They emphasize citizen-based politics within individual European nations – East and West – to secure democratic relations between citizens and their governments, and the need to increase contacts between people across frontiers of the political–military divide 'which separates us against our will'. The Chartists have always insisted that human rights and freedom must become a multinational concern: 'The happiness and freedom of mankind is indivisible and those who are capable of feeling concerned about the fate of the individual on earth cannot restrict such a responsibility by state frontiers and cannot be indifferent to what happens beyond them'. They have expressed solidarity with all those who suffer unjustly and with those who struggle 'for a happier life by means which respect the dignity and rights of the individual' in the East and in the West.

Most Chartists agree that the major obstacles they face stem from the undemocratic legacy of the last war, the division of Europe with which the nations of Central and Eastern Europe have never been reconciled. Their goal is a non-violent change of the political status quo and a democratic transformation of Europe into 'a pluralistic community of sovereign countries with equal rights'. It is therefore natural that they should seek contacts with groups that share this vision. Such contacts have led, since 1981, to an important, though controversial, dialogue with a section of the West European peace movement and to a realization of the need for the internationalization of civil movements. The jointly envisaged 'democratic and self-governing Europe' cannot, of course, ever become a reality without a major democratization of Central and Eastern Europe. The people of that area have for at least 40 years shared historical memories and political experiences. Their defeated individual revolts also made them aware that they need to learn from each other's mistakes and find a common solution. This outweighs their different traditions, nationalistic conflicts and past prejudices, and motivates their growing dialogue.

These mutual East European contacts have been obstructed, however, by their respective governments, which perceive a flow of people and information across their borders as a threat more serious than contacts across the Iron Curtain. It is no coincidence that many Hungarians are able to travel more freely to the West than to Czechoslovakia or Poland; that Czechs, Slovaks or East Germans cannot travel to many neighboring countries at all or only under strict restrictions, and so on. The reluctance of the authorities to promote the teaching of East European languages or the translation of their literature has to be perceived in this context.

Peter Uhl, an editor of one of the main Czech samizdat periodicals, *Informace o Charte 77* (Information on Charter 77), who spent nine years in prison for his convictions, recently told the *East European Reporter*: 'Governments are extraordinarily afraid of any coordination of resistance... The police [within the Soviet bloc] cooperate on all levels. In order to withstand their oppression and to overcome it we need to unite as well'.

CHARTER 77 AND THE POLES

The closest cooperation within the Soviet bloc has been achieved between the Czechs and the Poles. Systematic contact dates from summer 1978, when leading Chartists met with representatives of the Polish KOR in a mountainous border area and agreed on various forms of cooperation. Their third such meeting, in October 1978, was prevented by a joint Czechoslovak–Polish police action which resulted in the imprisonment of Jaroslav Sabata, a leading Chartist. Subsequent contacts had to take different forms. Although any mention of them has disappeared from the Western press, they have not ceased.

During the heyday of Solidarity in 1981, the Czechoslovak government unleashed a harsh repression. It was panicking that the 'Polish disease' might spill over to Czechoslovakia and give Charter 77 a role similar to KOR (sometimes described as Solidarity's midwife). The fact that conditions in Czechoslovakia made a battle for free trade unions a very unlikely prospect did not alter the authorities' real fear of it. The regime relaxed – although never to the pre-1980 level – only after the imposition of martial law.

Contacts among democratic opposition groups in the two countries have intensified since 1982. A number of joint Solidarity, KOR and Charter 77 statements have been made expressing support for common aims and the defense of each other's political prisoners, backed occasionally by hunger strikes or, in Poland, demonstrations. Samizdat books and periodicals are exchanged and the most important writings translated. New periodicals have emerged, devoted entirely to information about the neighboring country.

The Czech opposition's theoretical writing has begun to appear fairly systematically in Poland and has had a marked impact on a number of Solidarity leaders. Zbigniew Bujak, for example, explained that he and his friends were very impressed by Havel's essay, *Power of the Powerless*, and they tried to incorporate his analysis into their practice: 'Havel gave us the theoretical backing, a theoretical base for our actions. He enabled us to believe in their effectiveness. Until I read this text I was full of doubts'. Polish friends, especially in Wroclaw, have printed periodicals in Czech and smuggled them to Czechoslovakia together with other requested technical assistance. In July 1987 it was publicly acknowledged for the first time that since 1981 many of the contacts had been organized by a 'cooperation group' known as Polish–Czechoslovak Solidarity. Its confidence was demonstrated by naming two spokespersons – Anna Sabatova from Czechoslovakia and Josef Pinior from Poland – and by launching a new group, 'Circle of Friends of Polish–Czechoslovak Solidarity', which includes many leading Solidarity and Charter 77 activists.

The group is involved in the 'coordination of a diversity of international activities... in the context of wider relations between other independent groups in the countries of the Eastern bloc'. In August 1987, on the anniversary of the Warsaw Pact invasion of Czechoslovakia, 21 prominent Czechoslovak and Polish leaders, all of whom are among the declared members of the Circle of Friends of Polish–Czechoslovak Solidarity, met on the border and issued a joint statement on shared aims and basic ideals. These ideals are defined as: 'a deeper respect for human rights and a consequent reconstitution of the legal system and the legal code; a deeper respect for social rights including the right to found independent trade unions; the ideal of political pluralism and self-government; spiritual, cultural and religious freedom and tolerance; respect for national individuality and the rights of national minorities; the freedom to search for and create a better-functioning economic system which would provide a space for people's creativity and also for real responsibility of all workers for the results of their labor and their share of economic decision-making; and the ideal of a peaceful, democratic and environmentally-conscious Europe, as a friendly association of independent states and nations'.

Some of these statements echo the Appeal made in October 1986 on the 30th anniversary of the Hungarian Revolution, and the political document prepared jointly by independent human rights and peace activists from Eastern and Western Europe, known as the Memorandum and published in November 1986 under the title, *Giving Real Life to the Helsinki Accords*.

HUNGARIAN APPEAL

The Appeal commemorating the Hungarian Revolution was unprecedented because it was the first time representatives from democratic opposition groups from several East European countries formulated a common policy. The document, signed by 122 leading dissidents from Czechoslovakia, East Germany, Hungary and Poland, and subsequently endorsed by three Romanians, pledged 'joint determination to struggle for political democracy in our countries, their independence, pluralism based on the principles of self-management, peaceful reunification of divided Europe and its democratic integration, as well as for the rights of all minorities'. They emphasized 'support for one another in our current struggles for a better, more decent and freer life in our countries and the whole world'.

The initiative for such a joint action came from some editors of the Hungarian samizdat journal *Beszelo*, and discussions across borders about the wording of the text were facilitated by the London-based East European Cultural Foundation. In this way, the travel restrictions imposed on East European dissidents have been circumvented; one Hungarian had his passport confiscated because of his contacts with the Czechs and Poles. Another *Beszelo* editor, Miklos Haraszti, claimed that the joint declaration 'marked the beginning of a new era' because it highlighted 'new consciousness, clearer realization of the need to internationalize our common problems if we are ever to achieve a democratic Eastern Europe'. According to Haraszti, the previous individual national democratic renewals all failed to internationalize the crisis situation, and as the crisis will 'inevitably arise again we have to make sure that we will not again fail to evoke the international dimension'. This, of course, involved the need to explore the possibility of a joint approach to Moscow. Understandably, simultaneous pressure from movements for change in Poland, Czechoslovakia, Hungary and even East Germany would make it more difficult for the Soviet Union to apply its usual 'divide and conquer' rules and would narrow its room for maneuver, thereby improving the odds for an acceptable compromise.

The success of the 'Hungarian Appeal' led to discussions about the possibility of formulating 'a minimum common political program of the East European democratic opposition'. Many participants in these talks have agreed that to reach a consensus on such a program is not going to be easy, and that one fairly safe method is to reach an agreement on a series of concrete issues, situated within their appropriate political contexts, and eventually the basis for a common denominator should emerge. The first issues put forward for discussions are: lack of freedom of travel within the Soviet bloc; the need for a civilian alternative to military service, and the role of the army in a totalitarian country subordinated to the interests of a foreign power; and ecological problems and their political and sociological consequences. Several documents dealing with one or the other of these issues have already been produced by some of the individual national groups. They will serve as contributions to the discussions about the first draft of the joint statement. The concrete demands stemming from these three issues put forward by the Czechs and Poles in their above-mentioned August statement signaled a further stage in the complex process of adopting a joint East European position.

DIALOGUE WITH THE PEACE MOVEMENT

These issues were also included in the *Helsinki Memorandum*. Human rights and peace groups and individuals from more than a dozen countries in the East and West responded to the contents of the three Helsinki Final Act 'baskets' and suggested steps toward a more comprehensive détente. The Memorandum was inspired by the March 1985 *Prague Appeal*, in which leading Charter 77 signatories emphasized the importance of the Helsinki process for overcoming the division of Europe and argued that there will be no peace without the removal of this artificial barrier. Following year-long discussions – many of them heated and controversial – a consensus was reached. The resulting text incorporates many of the arguments expressed by the Polish *Freedom and Peace* group, by the East German *Peace and Human Rights* group, by members of the Hungarian democratic opposition, by a Slovenian peace group and especially by members of Charter 77.

The Memorandum's signatories (about 500 to date, half of them from Eastern Europe) declare their opposition to 'any tendency to play off peace against freedom or vice versa'. They make it clear that 'peace on our continent can only be secure if it is really a democratic peace [this term was first introduced by Charter 77 – JK], based on civil liberties and social justice. . . in our view the implementation of basic civil rights – such as freedom of thought and conscience, freedom of assembly and association, and freedom of information – is an ongoing condition: for societies to be able. . . to safeguard disarmament and a stable, lasting democratic peace on our continent'. In the concluding section they describe 'the Europe we envisage' as 'a pluralistic, democratic and peaceful community of nations acting as partners with equal rights [in which] all peoples have the possibility of organizing their mutual relations as well as their internal political, economic and cultural affairs in a democratic and self-determined way'.

The similarity with Charter 77 formulations is not a coincidence. Most of the ideas and measures put forward in the Memorandum had previously been raised in Charter 77 discussion papers. These included the withdrawal of all foreign weapons and troops from Europe, the dissolution of NATO and the Warsaw Pact and other bilateral and multilateral military treaties between Helsinki signatory states (perceived as a step toward the overcoming of the division of Europe) and a peace constitution for Europe based on full respect for the right of self-determination of all nations, which would transform the ten basic principles proclaimed in the Helsinki Accords into political reality.

The dialogue with the peace movements remains controversial, and Charter 77 spokespersons meticulously ensure that those Czechoslovak contributions which do not represent the views of the entire movement are presented as discussion papers expressing the opinions only of the authors and signatories. However, it should be noted that almost all such papers are signed by individuals who play a leading role within the Charter 77 community. Three-quarters of the Hungarian Appeal's signatories from Czechoslovakia signed the Memorandum, and the most well known of them also took part in the meeting on the Czechoslovak–Polish border.

Jiří Dienstbier argues that 'peace as we understand it can be permanently secured only through gradual elimination of social tensions'. He approvingly quotes the Ljubljana unofficial peace group argument that peace – between people and societies rather than between states – can be understood 'as abolition of borders between civil societies, as a factor in the internationalization of civil society' and he adds that 'civil society is fortified by every restriction of influence of the military and security forces'.

CHARTER 77 AND THE EAST GERMANS

Paradoxically, the dialogue with the Western peace movement helped to facilitate a closer cooperation with the East German peace and human rights movement, whose 'concrete aims' Charter 77 had already endorsed in April 1982.

The development of Soviet nuclear missiles in Czechoslovakia and the GDR intensified their dialogue. In November 1984 16 leading Charter 77 signatories and 13 leading East German activists issued a joint declaration appealing for a Europe free from missiles from the Urals to the Atlantic. Significantly, they stressed that the division of the world into blocs is the main cause of the current international crisis, rather than nuclear armament, an argument later elaborated upon in the *Prague Appeal*. The East Germans promptly endorsed the principles of the *Prague Appeal* and argued that the peace movement 'must be an emancipation movement in the widest sense. Ecology, Third World and women's groups belong to it, as do movements which work for the democratic renewal of society, for the establishment of human rights and for an alternative culture, as do social and national minorities. . .' It came as no surprise that the 44 East German signatories of the Memorandum had all (with one exception) signed the *Hungarian Appeal*', and that the launching documents of the new *Peace and Human Rights* group clearly echoed Charter 77 documents, and to an extent also those of the Polish *Freedom and Peace* group. The East German democratic and peace activists are determined to play an active role in coordination with other East European civil rights groups, despite the growing obstacles that they face.

CHARTER 77 AND THE HUNGARIANS

Contacts with activists of the Hungarian democratic opposition have also been developing for several years. There is no independent organization in Hungary comparable to Charter 77 or to Solidarity and Freedom and Peace, but Chartists have maintained contacts – principally with the editors of the samizdat periodical *Beszelo* and with the ecological group Danube Circle, which attempted to prevent or at least to diminish the adverse consequences of the joint Czechoslovak–Hungarian Danube dam project. Some of the exchanges were marked by tensions stemming from unsolved problems in Hungarian–Slovak relations. The Hungarian opposition is very sensitive about the treatment of Hungarian minorities abroad, and although Hungarians in Slovakia are not treated as badly as they are in Romania, they are still subjected to discrimination. At the same time, according to a number of Slovak Charter 77 intellectuals, the documents of the Hungarian opposition do not take into account or respond to the historical causes of this national conflict.

Recently, relations between the activists in the two countries have significantly improved. Charter 77 spokespersons published several documents concerning the suppression of the rights of the Hungarian minority in Slovakia and they also established close cooperation with the Committee for the

Defence of the Rights of the Hungarian Minority in Slovakia, led by Miklos Duray. Efforts taken to explore the possibilities of closer cooperation both on concrete, pressing issues and on long-term joint approaches enjoy the unequivocal support of both sides.

CONCLUSIONS

There is no blueprint for effecting change in the communist systems of Eastern and Central Europe. Those who believe that the system is reformable advocate different sets of political and economic reforms which can be implemented from either above or below. Czechoslovakia experienced reforms from above between 1963 and 1967 and at the beginning of 1968; the Soviet Union is currently being given a dose of them by Mikhail Gorbachev. The second method depends on rallying the membership of the communist party, the unions and so on, to attempt to democratize the structures from below. Some attempt at this was made during the 'Prague Spring' of 1968. Both methods introduce functional changes designed to modernize the political and economic system and make it more efficient, but the second can open the door to structural changes which in turn may lead to the emergence of a democratic system. Those who believe that the system is not reformable wish to achieve major structural changes by encouraging the growth of independent groups and social movements which promote fundamental values and reflect the real aspirations of the people.

This third concept is not incompatible with reform – especially not with reform from below – and under certain circumstances, as the Prague Spring experience has shown, the concepts can be complementary. Solidarity embraced this strategy, and the importance of its experience for other independent groups cannot be exaggerated. Different methods, in various combinations, have varying relevance in each East European country, and independent groups will therefore necessarily adopt – especially in the short term – tactics appropriate to their own situations. This obviously does not preclude the possibility of a future joint approach, and only serves to underline the need to share experiences, learn from each other's mistakes, improve mutual understanding and coordinate activities in order 'to create a fertile ground for possible future coordination of the struggle of these societies for greater freedom' (Havel).

The present informal cooperation across East European frontiers will undoubtedly continue, develop and become stronger despite the fact that the regimes will do their utmost to make it a difficult uphill struggle. Cooperation can only lead to the growth of *de facto* pluralism from below, which could pave the way for a gradual democratization of the Soviet bloc. This could facilitate the ending of the Cold War, which, in turn could further accelerate democratization.

The social movement, not only in Poland but also in Czechoslovakia, is now so strong that it could only be defeated, as Dienstbier argues, 'by the new and total repression which would stem out of a war atmosphere'. Many of the Chartists, therefore, are determined to continue their dialogue with sections of the Western peace movement, especially with groups critical of the European political status quo and its social tensions. Individuals, groups and political parties in the West which are not reconciled to the political consequences of the division of Europe should be the natural partners of the democratic opposition east of the Elbe. They should not only strongly protest any violation of international human rights covenants or the Helsinki Accords, which guarantees the opposition's right to exist; they should also explore ways of helping it make progress on the concrete issues it has already placed on its agenda. At the very least, they should do so out of enlightened self-interest, since the reduction in militarization and increased democratization of the Eastern bloc that would result would have a significant and beneficial effect on the rest of Europe – if not the world.

16 Dissent in Yugoslavia
Aleksa Djilas

Communism is terminally ill: as an ideology and as a political and economic system it has no future. Yet it is still kicking. The Soviet Union's ability and desire to expand are still enormous, and the death throes of its empire will last at least several decades, if not a whole century. Moreover, the temptation in many Third-World countries is to believe that the five-pointed red star offers a quick way out of poverty, oppression and despair.

Therefore, communism has to be taken seriously. Yet it is tempting to dismiss it, for it has not kept its promises and it has not reached its goals. History, which is a mass graveyard of gods that failed, would be hard put to provide another case in which the achievement is in such great contrast to the aspiration. Not only has communism made human beings unfree and in some cases even more unequal than they were before, but it has proved unable to provide for the basic needs, let alone the affluence, of the masses. It restrains innovation and creativity in science, literature and philosophy, and is in permanent opposition to new knowledge. It cannot invent new technologies, but primarily imitates and replicates them, often after acquiring them through theft. (You cannot make computers with a hammer, and if you harvest with a sickle you will have to import wheat.) Further, communism is incapable of creating beauty, be it in art and architecture or in design and fashion. Further still, it is without a sense of humor, for humor presupposes the ability to observe oneself from a critical distance. As a result, it is boring.

The Yugoslav communist system shares in differing degrees all these characteristics of communism and , inevitably, Yugoslavia is in crisis. Communist countries are always in crisis, if by 'crisis' we mean a state of affairs in which the economy is inefficient, the population dissatisfied and the rulers deeply insecure about the legitimacy of their power. But Yugoslavia is in crisis in another sense, too. In the last six to seven years things have not only been bad, but have been getting worse.

The standard of living, for example, has fallen by roughly one third, the foreign debt is over $20 billion and unemployment is 17 per cent. Already more than a million Yugoslavs, primarily industrial workers and their families, live outside Yugoslavia, mostly in Western Europe. Workers' strikes are on the increase, while the ruling communist bureaucracies of the six 'socialist republics' and two 'autonomous socialist provinces' which constitute Yugoslavia cannot agree about common policies.

Parallel with the crisis, and partly as a reaction to it, a dissident movement has developed. Although its growth has been fast, of the six republics and two provinces only Slovenia and Serbia have dissident movements which can be considered a political force. (There are primarily concentrated in the capitals Ljubljana and Belgrade.)

In Slovenia there are almost no political prisoners, which is unique in the history of world communism since 1917. The press and media, when compared to those of Eastern Europe, are astonishingly open. Dissent in Slovenia is thus developing in favorable circumstances. Instead of being in direct conflict with the communist party, the dissidents often appear as a more radical version of the reformist groups in the party. The situation in Serbia is not as favorable as in Slovenia, yet the authorities are usually reluctant to impose prison sentences on dissidents. Also, many writers and historians are not afraid to give critical re-interpretations to events of the party's past. For example, the World War II struggle of the Yugoslav partisans, led by the communist party against the Germans and Italians and those Yugoslavs who collaborated with them, is now often analyzed as a complex mixture of war and civil war in which communists, although undoubtedly the most effective anti-fascist force, were also a revolutionary organization struggling for power.

Since the death of President Tito in May 1980, the activities and demands of dissidents in Ljubljana and Belgrade have been numerous, varied and far-reaching. In order to prevent further perversion of justice through politics, they have demanded an end to the party's domination over the courts, calling for an independent judiciary and greater respect for legal procedures. Then there was a petition for the abolition of the paragraph of the Yugoslav Criminal Code which prohibits the free expression of critical political views and opinions, defining them as 'enemy propaganda', and another petition for the right of workers to form free trade unions. They also called for accountability of high ranking party functionaries and free elections with candidates of differing political views.

Many Yugoslavs are deeply humiliated by the continuing official celebrations of Tito's birthday on 25 May, and by the running of a relay across Yugoslavia with a baton said to be carrying birthday greetings to Tito from the peoples of Yugoslavia. In Slovenia, signatures for a petition to abolish this extreme expression of personality cult were collected openly in streets and squares, and a few thousand people signed.

The Presidency of Yugoslavia was also petitioned to give amnesty to all political prisoners and to abolish the death penalty. In Yugoslavia capital punishment is not frequently used. However, many dissidents see the death penalty as a form of intimidation, since the Criminal Code permits it for so many crimes and in such an inexplicit and all-encompassing way that execution could even be used against some forms of non-violent, democratic opposition to the Yugoslav communist regime. For example, the Criminal Code states that 'creating and leading a counterrevolutionary organization which endangers the constitutional order' can carry capital punishment. These were precisely the words the Serbian Deputy Minister of the Interior used in an interview he gave in 1982 to describe my own activities. All I had done was write and edit some articles, journals and books in London.

What do these and many other petitions, demands, protest and appeals have in common? They are all requests for the introduction of liberal-democratic reforms in Yugoslavia. Although many signatories are former communists, there is no trace of Marxism-Leninism either in what they demand or in the arguments they use. The Soviet Union and other communist countries, in those rare cases when they are mentioned, are used only as negative examples. They are never held up as worth emulating or as societies of the future. Western European countries and the United States are not idealized, but it is openly acknowledged that in the realm of human rights they still have the highest standards in the world.

There should be not doubt that the large majority of Yugoslav dissidents consider communism a failure. They believe that it must be reformed, and by 'reform' they mean its transformation into liberal democracy. They do not want to reform it in the way in which Gorbachev is trying to reform the Soviet Union, namely to adapt it to the conditions of the modern industrial world while preserving its essence – the party's power monopoly.

If they were implemented, the reforms which the dissidents are demanding would ultimately abolish the party's monopoly of power. This is what most of them would dearly like to see happen. Only a small minority, however, would wish to ban the communist party from some future liberal-democratic Yugoslavia.

Dissent in Yugoslavia is committed to non-violence. Dissidents are not only against the violence which the state sometimes uses or threatens to use against its critics, but also against any violent methods of struggle for democratic reforms. Of course, any dissident statement which mentioned the need for a revolutionary transformation of Yugoslav society, let alone advocated violence, would be used by the authorities to crack down on the dissident movement. But the dissidents do not reject violence for tactical reasons or because they are afraid. Their opposition to violence is a sincere conviction, defended with as much dedication in private conversations as in public pronouncements.

This rejection of violence can only partly be explained as an expression of the dissidents' respect for the rights and life of the individual. It is a reflection of their abhorrence for human suffering. The other reasons are the still-living memories of the civil war that took place in Yugoslavia during World War II, and the fear that any violent political action could lead to conflicts between the different nations of Yugoslavia.

As in Eastern Europe, the dissident movement in Yugoslavia is dominated by intellectuals, many of whom are veteran opponents of the ruling system. The dissident voice, although intense in Ljubljana and Belgrade, is barely audible outside these two cities, and the influence of dissidents on the working class is still very small.

Dissent in Eastern Europe in the 1970s and 1980s has been largely unsuccessful. This does not mean that the efforts of the dissidents have been in vain, or that they should not have engaged in their activities. It would be a grave intellectual error, and an even greater moral one, to look down contemptuously on dissidents as 'failures'. The ethical message which they have conveyed is of immeasurable value, and it will prove an enduring investment in the future of their peoples. Dissent in Eastern Europe has been, therefore, unsuccessful simply in the sense that the respect for human rights and the increase in the freedom of the individual that the dissidents have demanded has not been achieved.

The two most important causes of the defeat of dissent in Eastern Europe have been Soviet interference in internal affairs, underscored by the threat of Soviet invasion, and the 'monolithic' opposition of communist parties to fundamental changes. Yugoslavia is in a better position than some of the other countries. There is no Soviet control (and only an indirect threat of Soviet tanks rolling across the border), and the Yugoslav communists, although most unwilling to give up power, are still reluctant to suppress the demands for liberal-democratic reforms. Most dissidents are aware that there are many moderates and reformists in the party, and that these communists are in conflict with hard-line Titoists who want to preserve the system at all costs.

Will the Yugoslav dissidents succeed where the other Eastern European dissidents have failed and, for the first time in history, transform a communist system into a liberal-democratic one? The fact that important liberal-democratic changes have already taken place in Yugoslavia, without any violence and upheaval, gives reason for hope. Also, since these changes were not planned in advance and came both from 'above' and from 'below', they are obviously supported by many people. The absence of a leading political figure who can be identified with them is a good thing, too, since it means that their future does not depend on his political survival or change of mood. Yet although the scope of freedom has increased considerably, the League of Communists of Yugoslavia (as the communist party is officially called) still has the monopoly of power. In order to transform the achieved liberties into genuine liberal democracy, an organized mass movement with clearly-defined political goals, similar to Solidarity in Poland, would be necessary. But the multinational structure of Yugoslavia makes the creation of an all-Yugoslav liberal-democratic mass movement extremely difficult. In this respect, it is encouraging to see examples of cooperation and solidarity among dissident groups of different nationalities. For example, Belgrade dissidents often demand the release of political prisoners in other republics, even those accused of expressing opinions which are critical of the Serbian nation. Though still infrequent, this kind of readiness of the Serbs to listen to the grievances – whether justified or not – of non-Serbs is important, since it promises that the creation of liberal democracy would also bring about a peaceful and civilized dialogue between the representatives of the different nations of Yugoslavia.

17 Cultural Resistance: Parallel Literature in Czechoslovakia

Jan Vladislav

The award of the 1984 Nobel Prize for literature to Czech poet Jaroslav Seifert caught Western journalists napping. Their scramble for information provided concrete proof of the free world's ignorance of what used to be called Central Europe and is now regarded as part of Eastern Europe. More disturbing, however, is that in many cases people do not appreciate just how uninformed they are and do not hesitate to express opinions. A well-known Parisian weekly, for example, made the 'expert' pronouncement that the Swedish Academy was not honoring a poet but a dissident whose greatest literary achievement had been to sign Charter 77.

Of course, ignorance of the literature of a little country in the middle of Europe is, in itself, nothing unusual. What is rather more worrying, however, is that the lack of knowledge in this field is symptomatic of a dramatic, *overall* ignorance not restricted solely to culture. Furthermore, because the particular nature of Central Europe's historical development has meant that culture has always played a major role in political affairs, it is impossible without sufficient knowledge of the cultural factor to have any clear picture of the historical and political development of the Czechs and Slovaks. This applies not just to the last century, when it was a question of preserving their threatened languages as well as their cultural and national identities, but also to the first decades of this century, when it was a matter of creating and preserving the first Czechoslovak state of modern times. It applies equally to the entire past half-century, which encompasses the German occupation, the intermezzo of 1945–47, the 1948 takeover, the Stalinism of the fifties and the slight relaxation in the sixties which culminated in the Prague Spring of 1968 and terminated with the Soviet occupation and the 'normalization' which still prevails.

Quite simply, for almost two centuries now, the history of Czech and Slovak culture has been an inseparable part of Czechoslovak history as a whole. However, over the past 50 years its importance has assumed a whole new dimension, since it has mirrored more clearly than anything else those aspects of Czech and Slovak reality which historians, for various reasons, either ignore or suppress. Official Czech historiography all too often contents itself with a superficial account – what one might call the official version – of events past and present. By and large it reduces history to a succession of power struggles, revolutions, governments, party congresses, trials, convictions and even rehabilitations: in short, it is the history of the ruling minority. History conceived in this manner has no room for the history of the ruled and of the 'silenced majority' which is just as significant, to say the least. We must look elsewhere for a picture of that hidden face of modern Czech and Slovak history, and most of all to independent literature which, though still suppressed, is very much alive.

Incidentally, one need look no further than to the case of Jaroslav Seifert for a vivid illustration of this unintended though inevitable conjunction of culture and politics in the history of the Czechs and Slovaks. Seifert was certainly no political poet by any means, and from the end of the twenties he tended to stay away from the intense political involvement of most of his literary friends. His poetry is first and foremost an intimate celebration of love and life, in short, of 'all the beauties of the earth' as the emblematic title of his Memoirs reminds us. However, this outlook did not prevent Seifert from speaking his mind about the burning issues of the day whenever he thought it necessary. He did so to enormous effect in a series of poems just before the war, as well as during the German occupation, when he literally became a national poet. He did so in Spring 1956, with his speech at the Second Czechoslovak Writers' Congress, where he spoke out boldly in favor of the political and moral renewal of society. And he did so at the time of Prague Spring, in spite of illness and old age, and during the subsequent normalization, when he became one of the leading exponents of the so-called 'unofficial' or 'parallel' culture.

Jaroslav Seifert was not alone in this respect, of course. By and large, the Western public fails to realize that the overwhelming majority of Czech and Slovak books published in the West in translation over the past decades were banned from publication in Czechoslovakia because they belonged to the unofficial, parallel cultural scene which is, by definition, prohibited and used by the regime as a pretext to repress not only writers, but also those who copy, distribute or merely read their works. [Of course, things have dramatically changed fro the better after Czechoslovakia's 'velvet revolution' in November 1989. The once banished authors are now prominent public figures, and Vaclav Havel is the country's President. (Eds)]

The complete list of banned books would run to dozens of printed pages and would include a large number of leading works of present-day Czech and Slovak literature. For the sake of illustration, we may mention some of them, such as Josef Škvorecký's celebrated novel, *Tankovy prapor* (The Tank Battalion). Although the book was written in the early fifties and has appeared with success in several world languages, it has yet to be published in Czechoslovakia and circulates there solely in typewritten copies or exile editions. A similar fate is shared by several of Bohumil Hrabal's major prose works. The authentic versions of these also appeared only in translation, and Czech readers know their full version solely in samizdat form or from exile editions. This is because the 'official' editions of the author's work suffered as a result both of state censorship and the writer's own self-censorship. In the seventies many more names joined the list of unofficial authors, including Ludvik Vaculik, Pavel Kohout, Ivan Klima, Jan Trefulka and Milan Kundera. Their novels often appeared in translation than in the original Czech and were accessible in the home country only in typecopy or in exile publications. This fate is suffered not only by Czech prose and poetry, but also by drama. The case of Vaclav Havel, of course, is particularly known: those of his plays written after 1970 are performed and published throughout the free world, but in Czechoslovakia they continue to be banned and circulate solely in samizdat or exile editions.

The aforementioned authors and works are only the tip of the proverbial iceberg, the bulk of which is submerged and therefore invisible. One could cite dozens of other writers who have been banned from official publication either since 1948 or 1970 and hundreds of books which have been created over that period and are available to Czechoslovak readers at best in samizdat form. One could also cite many other fields in which significant works have been written but circulate in their country of origin solely in the form of typewritten copies, even when they are published in several languages abroad and enjoy signal success there. Let us recall such varied works as the political essays of Milan Simecka, the studies of literary history by the late Vaclav Cerny (not to mention his Memoirs) or the philosophical writings of Jan Patocka, which have either been published or are due to be published in German, French and English.

This outline of the present state of Czech and Slovak parallel literature is not exhaustive, of course. Its aim is merely to give some sense of the extent and significance of the phenomenon, as well as of its history, which is quite different from, and much longer than as usually presented. There are some authors, including Milan Kundera, who have a tendency to situate the beginning of Czech and Slovak spiritual resistance – and hence of the independent activity now known as unofficial or parallel culture – at the beginning of the seventies. This is largely due to their personal experience: they themselves were first involved in this activity after the Prague Spring and the Soviet occupation of 1968, when they were disbarred from the official culture of which they were formerly a part.

In reality, the history of Czech – and in certain cases Slovak – spiritual resistance goes back to the communist takeover of February 1948. At that time a considerable number of intellectuals, university teachers, students and artists were excluded from public activity as a result of harsh administrative measures. Many of them, including two score of the country's writers, were jailed in the fifties, while a still greater number were deprived of any opportunity to work within their chosen disciplines. Numerous authors were expelled from the official Writer's Union and lost all chance of being published. Czechoslovak intellectuals virtually split into two camps at that time: on the one hand, there were those who accepted the cultural policies of the new regime, whether out of conviction or opportunism; on the other, there were those who, in one way or another, realized the danger facing the spiritual identity of every individual and of the national society as a whole, and sought to confront it by continuing to work according to the dictates of their conscience, with no prospect of public expression.

One outcome of that situation was that a whole number of books came into being, including those we have already noted. Most of these manuscripts were read and passed around more or less spontaneously among friends and acquaintances. In the case of Jiři Kolar, one of his manuscripts was confiscated by the police at a friend's home, which led to the poet being prosecuted and sentenced to a year's imprisonment. Many other manuscripts circulated in like manner among friends and acquaintances, such as the poems of the long-imprisoned poet Jan Zahradniček, a series of collections by young surrealist writers, and the collection *Rozhovory* (Conversations) published at the beginning of his career by Vaclav Havel, together with a group of his friends – to mention but a few. Listing and evaluating the many books which were written and read, but not published, will be among the tasks facing those who write the detailed history of the Czech and Slovak intellectual resistance of the fifties.

Unhappily, such a history has yet to be written. But when it is, one fact that will undoubtedly emerge is that what is described in Czechoslovakia as independent or parallel culture is not merely a legacy of the Prague Spring of 1968 but actually a continuation of the spiritual resistance of the fifties. In the course of 'normalization in the seventies and eighties, that resistance naturally assumed new dimensions. Above all, it led to a new distribution of forces. Following the purges in education, the press and culture, thousands upon thousands of intellectual workers were excluded from public activity, including hundreds of journalists and writers who had taken part, as party members, in the renewal process of the sixties. The French poet Louis Aragon dubbed that merciless purge 'a spiritual Biafra'. However, it was in fact essentially a replay of the purges which afflicted Czech and Slovak culture in the wake of 1948. In any case, it served to reinforce Czech and Slovak intellectual resistance not only in terms of numbers but also experience, particularly experience gained within the regime's own structures.

The 'normalization' of the seventies also engendered a change of outlook. In the fifties Czech and Slovak spiritual resistance was geared toward an eventual relaxation of regime pressure, and events were to vindicate such an approach. During the seventies, in the light of the new experiences, the resistance quickly realized that prospects for a change within the regime were unlikely and it was therefore vital to work either on the fringes of the official structures or entirely outside them. This outlook was given theoretical expression by Vaclav Benda in his 1978 essay, *Paralelni polis* (The parallel polis), and above all by Vaclav Havel in his celebrated essay, *Moc bezmocnych* (The Power of the Powerless), of the same period. In everyday practice, such attitudes had already taken concrete form in the mushrooming of self-help publishing initiatives – what we know as *samizdat*. As time went by, the first book series, *Edice Petlice* (Padlock Books), founded and administered by Ludvik Vaculik, was joined by a whole series of other typewritten editions, from *Edice expedice* which is run by Vaclav Havel to *Kvart* (Quarto Press), which I myself managed until my departure into exile. We should also mention the philosophical series, *Nove cesty mysleni* (New Thought Trails) and other collections of specialized literature, which include both original writing and translations of foreign works. At first, the samizdat publishers brought out texts which had been rejected by 'normalization' censors or which had awaited publication since the fifties or sixties. In time, however, writers from the parallel cultural scene started writing directly for samizdat. This turned out to be a decisive step toward a new level of freedom, in that they ceased to care about the possibility of official publication and no longer felt above them the Damoclean sword of censorship – above all, self-censorship. The upshot are books which, irrespective of differences of language, subject-matter, genre and quality, have one thing in common: a growing degree of internal freedom.

Czech and Slovak parallel literature is literature like any other. It encompasses the outstanding, the mediocre and even the dreadful. It does not regard itself as an élite category. It does not demand particular recognition, nor does it strive for any special status: that was imposed on it by the present regime. Parallel literature came into being for practical reasons: it aims to create a link between writers, who were arbitrarily excluded from publishing, and readers, who were cut off from an important component of their national literature. It does not have any fixed unifying program, either artistic or political. Its sole ambition is to keep what Milan Simecka refers to as a pluralist literature. It represents a bulwark against the encroaching reduction of thought and language which in totalitarian systems always threatens to turn into Orwellian *Newspeak*. It is a self-defense mechanism against the offensive mounted by the totalitarian regime against the diversity of human life, since such an offensive is 'not just an attack on one facet or area of life but on life as a whole' (Vaclav Havel in *Priben a totalita* [Story and totalitarianism]). In the final analysis, parallel literature is one of the most important means of helping to preserve the hard-pressed individual and collective memory and identity of the Czechs and Slovaks. Therein lay its profound *raison d'être* from the very first. Therein lies still its unifying mission for the future.

18 Ethnic Dissent In Eastern Europe: The Romanian– Hungarian Conflict
Geza Szöcs

According to a time-worn anecdote, impossible to verify, in 1941, when war was officially declared between Hungary and the United States, President Roosevelt posed the following questions to his Deputy Secretary of State:

'Does Hungary hold any territorial demands against us?'
'None, Mr President.'
'Then against which country does it hold them?'
'Against Romania, Mr. President.'
'So Hungary has now declared war on Romania too?'
'No, begging your pardon. In this war, Romania is an ally of Hungary.'

The story, if apocryphal, is useful because it sheds light on a peculiar, tragicomic set of circumstances: despite the differences which separate the two countries, Romania and Hungary were once allies on the side of the Axis powers during World War II.

Since the situation today is similar, if not entirely analogous, the anecdote leads us to ask a crucial question: up to what point can these two countries remain allies, even ostensibly, and continue to be run along the same, or more or less parallel course of communism, when they exhibit such vastly different expressions of this same ideology? Ultimately, we must answer another question: are their two paths destined to collide? Is it conceivable that at some future date these two countries will find themselves at war with one another? [Written in 1987, this essay reflects enduring and legitimate fears. Following the Romanian Christmas Revolution (December 1989) relations between the two nations have improved, but one should not dismiss the threat of resurgent ethnic strife. Recent tensions in Transylvania have shown that the roots of this conflict go way back in history. Although the political setting in both Romania and Hungary has changed lately, some of the topics addressed by this contributor remain quite disturbing. (Eds)]

Today, Romania and Hungary comprise the two most dissimilar societies in the Warsaw Pact. Though neighbors geographically, this serves only to heighten the tensions between them. One of them, Hungary, in 1956 waged a heroic and unsuccessful struggle against the Soviet troops which continue to this day to occupy the country. By contrast, the Russians voluntarily withdrew from Romania in 1958. What followed was the emergence of an allegedly independent Romanian foreign policy, widely acclaimed until recently by Western politicians.

Further contrasts between the two countries are easy to identify: within the region, Hungary enjoys the highest stand-ard of living, while Romania is often called the 'Ethiopia of Europe'. Hungary's economic policies can be considered the most liberal within the Eastern bloc, while the super-centralization carried out in Romania accounts for the near total ruin of its economy. Human rights violations are the fewest in Hungary, while Romania was until the recent revolu-tion a dark police state whose society was permeated through and through by a kind of Narodnik-style National-Socialism with Byzantine overtones. Hungary belongs to the hard core of the Warsaw Pact, while Romania is a looser adherent. Hungary's foreign policy is most often a faithful maidservant to the Soviet master, while Romania still claims to follow a more independent course. Having listed these contrasting elements, the question remains: do these elements amount to *conflicts* or only *differences* between the two countries?

There does exist a source of tension between the two states which can be regarded as an irreconcilable conflict of interest. It is the problem of the two million Hungarians living in Transylvania. During the decades following World War II, the successive regimes in Hungary exhibited a conspicuous disregard – deemed criminal by domestic public opinion – for the fate of the millions of Hungarians living under Romanian rule. Recently, however, a perceptible change of course has taken place in the conduct of Hungarian foreign policy – and to some degree even in domestic policy. The political leadership in Budapest now displays a greater sense of responsibility toward the Hungarians of Transylvania, including the thousands of refugees who escaped the former Ceausescu regime and settled in Hungary. Even at international forums, Hungarian officials are beginning to raise their voice in defense of the rights of Transylvanian Hungarians.

Let us review the factors which have contributed to changing Hungarian policy to a point that it seems willing to risk an open break in relations with Romania. First, there is the unsurpassed brutality with which the Romanian government sought to denationalize, forcibly assimilate, and otherwise compel the disappearance of the country's national minorities – including not just Hungarians, but Germans, Serbs and Jews as well. Second, unlike Romania, leadership changes in Hungary have, over time, resulted in the removal of Stalinist cadres whose behavior was governed by knee-jerk adherence to a misinterpreted dogma of socialist internationalism. Third, various pressures felt by the Hungarian government have worked to compel its recent change of heart on the minority issue. Among these pressures were:

(a) The growing resistance to political oppression by minority Hungarians themselves, especially in Transylvania, but in Slovakia as well. This resistance has received increasing international attention. The underground, samizdat activity of Miklós Duray (in Czechoslovakia) and Karoly Kiraly and the independent journal *Ellenpontok* (in Romania) have had the effect of exposing to Hungarian society the serious and unresolved fate of Hungarian minorities living in neighboring states. As a result, the Hungarian leadership could have avoided these matters only at the cost of great loss to its prestige.

(b) Minority resistance coincided with the demands and efforts of Hungarians in the West, and served to increase the credibility, prestige and influence of those efforts.

This question leads us to ponder the future of the region as a whole. One of the most important questions for Gorbachev in terms of both domestic and foreign policy is whether the Soviet leadership has the courage to side with the majority. By *majority*, of course, I mean the *minorities*. We know, after

all, that national minorities in the Soviet Union comprise
more than 50 per cent of the population. Nothing would win
Gorbachev greater popularity (albeit a precarious popularity)
than if he espoused the protection of nationality interests in
an open, consistent and effective fashion. Such a move would
create a new situation not only within the Soviet Union but
in southeastern Europe as well.

Moving beyond the southeast European context, a lib-
eralized nationality policy along the lines outlined above
would upgrade the credibility of the Soviet regime, and of
communism in general, in all those centuries where one or
another Soviet national minority (Jewish, German, and so on)
comprises the majority. It would gain sympathy among the
Armenian diaspora scattered around the world. It would win
the support of the entire *fourth world*, that is, among those
nationalities which can be expected, within the next 30 years
or so, to attain a considerably higher level of self-awareness
and political organization. Whatever else happens, this evolutionary development will significantly alter the balance of
forces not only within individual states, but among the various
countries in the international arena as well. The communist
system, if it acknowledged these realities, could avoid the
brunt of the social and political conflicts which are certain
to arise.

Nationalism in the Romanian context also means that the
only way the present leadership can hold this impoverished
society together is through a rhetoric whose end result is some
form of aggressive expansionism. The formula is an age-old
one, last seen at work in Argentina. Romania's Malvinas
Islands is none other than Transylvania, the only difference
being that Romania *already possesses* this province. Be that
as it may, the country behaves as if it had to remain in a
constant state of military preparedness for war in the cause
of Transylvania.

The above are introductory ruminations. The conclusions
that they imply can be summed up as follows:

(1) Neither communism, as the commonly espoused, official
ideology, nor the fact of membership in the same military camp should be regarded as obstacles to potential war
between Romania and Hungary.

(2) The Soviet Union, by reforming its minority policies,

would have the means to find a satisfactory solution to the nationality problems of the entire region. If it were able to institute such reforms – of which there is no prospect, at present – the West would fall behind in the area.

(3) So long as there are superpower forces whose interest is to continue to preserve peace in Europe, there is no possibility of armed conflict between the two countries.

(4) In the event of large-scale, conventional warfare in Europe, it is a virtual certainty that Hungary and Romania would end up on opposite sides, regardless of where they started out.

(5) Contrary to popular opinion, it is unlikely that Hungary and Romania will jointly and voluntarily participate in any kind of regional confederation. The only conceivable framework would be a kind of 'United States of Europe'. Short of that, there is little chances for integration of any kind in Eastern Europe, whether communist-sponsored or non-communist.

(6) The political conditions prevailing in Romania make it impossible to regard unofficial movements as bearing any real significance. Their influence on domestic political conditions is minuscule and is unlikely to grow in the future. In the same vein, efforts to secure minority rights have failed to have any impact on the Romanian government's minority policy; their only effect was on the Hungarian government, insofar as they have contributed to the change in that government's policy toward Romania.

In closing, we may comment that Eastern Europe's place in the intellectual and political world can best be characterized as antipodean. While the center of intellectual and technological civilization shifts more and more to the West, the political mores and conditions forced upon Eastern Europe come further and further from the East. Our world is governed by political strategies born in the taigas of Eastern Siberia, and electronic devices from California and Japan. The scissors have opened so wide that perhaps sometime soon the blades will meet somewhere in the Pacific Ocean. At the moment, Eastern Europe falls at the greatest distance, both geographically and intellectually, from the point where decisions of consequence are made.

That the nationality question remains unresolved does not

mean simply that it has not been solved, but rather suggests functional disorders in the political structure. These disorders may result in the eruption of conflicts worldwide. Nationality conflicts were the root cause of two world wars. We have been witness to a variety of murderous peace treaties, revolutions, counter-revolutions, foreign occupations and massive deportations – yet the classical seats of hatred in Eastern Europe have only grown more infected. The only elements missing to make the region ready for an apocalypse were communist aggression and the Iron Curtain. To date, communism has failed – in Eastern Europe as well – to secure the long-term interests of any larger nationality. The conclusion is unequivocal: if this remains unchanged, the prospects for the survival of communism can only diminish.

Part IV
Intellectuals and the
Communist State

19 Cooperation and Conflict
Paul Hollander

The relationship between intellectuals and communist systems has a complicated and stormy history. This is true both
as regards intellectuals who live under such systems and those
who 'relate' to such systems from a safe distance. We may
propose that a crucial determinant of such a relationship is
the degree of proximity between the intellectuals and the communist systems: the further away the intellectuals, the more
benign the attitudes on both sides and the more agreeable the
relationship. Furthermore, the longer the communist system
has been in existence the more strained the relationship
between the system and the resident intellectuals.

The ranks that follow address only the relationship between
communist systems and the intellectuals who live under
them. (I have addressed the issue of the relationship between
non-resident, primarily Western, intellectuals and communist
states elsewhere, see Hollander 1981, 1983). In discussing
intellectuals and communist systems, the central questions
are: what impact do such states have on intellectuals and, in
turn, what influence do intellectuals have on these political
systems and their future and possible transformation? What
we may conclude about this relationship – and about the role
of intellectuals in the persistence or change of communist
states – will in large measure depend on our understanding
of who these intellectuals are and how we define the subject
of the discussion. My own view is that intellectuals have
been and should be perceived as social critics and value-
formulating élites: producers and interpreters of ideas, but
ideas of a more general, that is, social, cultural or political
nature. Intellectuals can be legitimizers or servants of the
status quo, but more often than not they are critics, especially
when they have a choice. They do not have much choice when
the alternative to being a legitimizer is the certitude of puni-
tive sanctions which may range from the loss of occupation

to exile and imprisonment. When such risks are faced, one cannot expect intellectuals to embrace the social–critical role in significant numbers.

It follows that intellectuals, or most of them, cannot help but cease to be intellectuals in closed societies in which they are forced to abandon what is central to the traditional Western conception of intellectuals, namely the critical role. As I have written elsewhere, I believe that 'Today people who used to be called philosophers are called intellectuals; they do what philosophers were supposed to do: reflect, meditate, or pontificate in private and public on a more or less full time basis on the great issues of life and death, society and the individual, things timely and timeless'.[1]

Obviously, in communist societies it is difficult to live up to this notion of the intellectual and especially to perform such activities in public.

There are other views held about intellectuals (or the intelligentsia) in communist societies. Churchward's discussion of Soviet intellectuals (among others) does not rest on a perception of them as free spirits and unfettered social critics. He writes: 'most Soviet intellectuals. . . are prepared to work within the Communist political system, to observe its rules and to respect its restraints'. He describes 'The basic role of the Soviet intelligentsia. . . to provide high-level specialists for all branches of human endeavor, including government and administration'. Moreover, 'Soviet intellectuals play an important role in the general process of political legitimation'. Still more crucial in his view is that 'a clear distinction cannot be drawn between intellectuals and the apparatchiki'.[2] He obviously differs from Sidney Monas who, following the earlier tradition, defines intellectuals as 'a spiritual brotherhood bearing a special burden of conscience'.[3]

The literature on intellectuals in communist systems is not extensive. (Among the small number of relevant works see Milosz, 1955; Aczel-Meray, 1960; Konrád-Szelenyi, 1979; Haraszti, 1987; Goldman, 1981 and 1987; partly relevant are such works as Leites, 1953; Djilas, 1957; Markov, 1984; Tismaneanu, 1988). Presumably, the relative scarcity of such writings is connected with the widespread assumption that there have hardly been any real intellectuals left in such closed societies and those surviving have not been able to function as intellectuals.

It has been justifiably held that intellectuals can partake of their distinctive activities only under an unusual combination of circumstances. There has to be a critical mass sufficiently numerous to generate a distinctive discourse; they need a tolerant culture that guarantees free expression and some degree of institutional protection and autonomy; they must also be able to make a living compatible with some freedom from routines that allows time and energy for critical reflection and unorthodox, inquisitive thinking.

'True intellectuals' of earlier generations became largely extinct in communist states of long standing such as the Soviet Union; they were mercilessly harassed and repressed in China under Mao; in Cuba they can still earn long prison sentences for possessing or circulating unauthorized manuscripts[4] (see, for example, Ripoll, 1985 and 1986). The ranks of such intellectuals have also been thinned out by emigration or exile, as witness the high proportion of intellectuals among former Soviet, Chinese, Hungarian, Czechoslovak and Cuban citizens in the West.

Generally speaking, intellectuals in communist states have had two major choices. They can maintain a critical and inde- pendent position and face the attendant risks and threats (ranging from loss of employment to loss of life) – or they can abandon the intellectual calling as earlier understood and offer their services to the party. More recently in some communist countries intellectuals have been able to opt for the critical role without facing *serious* retributions; the authorities in countries like Hungary, Poland and, to some extent, the Soviet Union now allow such intellectuals to maintain a precarious and truly marginal existence making a living from Western royalties or part-time jobs.

More typically, the non-conforming minority has been permitted to eke out a meager existence by menial laboring jobs, as distinguished writers have in Czechoslovakia or dissident scientists (including those applying for an exit visa) have in the Soviet Union, becoming janitors or laboratory technicians. In China during the Cultural Revolution, the handling of manure was favored by the authorities for those aspiring to the role of independent and critical intellectual (often even for those who did not have such an aspiration). In more tolerant

Hungary under Kádár, the government was content to deprive critical intellectuals of secure regular employment, especially academic.

For those intellectuals less concerned with preserving their traditional attributes and role and not anxious to take seemingly Quixotic positions there has been another option: to become functionaries, mental technicians assisting the ruling party and the State. For a small number who could at an earlier stage in their lives claim an intellectual calling, the transformation from independent social critic into revolutionary activist and later into party functionary was genuinely voluntary. In China, they '. . . . shared [Mao's] commitment to a Marxism-Leninism diffused with faith in the power of the will and the revolutionary consciousness to remold reality'.[5] In Eastern Europe such committed intellectuals '. . . . were perfectly equipped to understand the duplicity of the system and thus turn into its most ardent critics. At the same time they were emotionally involved in the adventure of power and could not find the resource to break with the mesmerizing ideological totems'.[6]

If one finds the political role of the functionary intellectual compatible with the original notion of what an intellectual is, then there is much to be said about the part played by intellectuals in communist societies: the functionary intellectuals have provided indispensable services to these systems as propagandists, educators and media specialists.

Although I myself to a narrower and more traditional conception of what an intellectual is, I think it is possible and useful to separate intellectuals in communist societies into three groups:

(1) The 'true intellectuals': independent, critical, autonomous, non-conformist dissenters such as Sakharov in the Soviet Union, Vaclav Havel (now President) in Czechoslovakia, Miklós Haraszti in Hungary, Milovan Djilas in Yugoslavia and their numerous imprisoned, exiled or unemployed colleagues;

(2) Functionary intellectuals: in particular, full-time party employees specializing in agitprop activities (broadly defined). They include officials, journalists, educators, establishment writers and social scientists dealing with ideas and social, cultural and political issues from the official point of view;

(3) Specialized, highly-skilled mental workers who are neither dissenters nor functionaries but apolitical experts or specialists (often in the sciences, industry or planning).

The generalizations to be made about the part played by intellectuals in communist societies depend on which of these three groups we focus on, in which countries and in what historical period.

It should be added that these categories are not immutable and impermeable; some intellectuals move from the conforming-supporting role to the dissenting-critical one (or vice versa), as, for example, did Georg Lukacs and many of his lesser-known compatriots, including the formerly loyal writers grouped around the weekly *Irodálmi Ujság (Literary Gazette)*, which became the major voice of social–political criticism before and during the 1956 revolution in Hungary. Early in their careers, many of them were independent social critics who subsequently became legitimizers. They ended up in the ranks of dissenters when no longer capable of rationalizing and tolerating the conflict between 'theory and practice'.

Historically, most intellectuals in communist states have belonged either to the functionary or the apolitical-expert category; the openly non-conformist group have usually been a small minority, given the risks and hardships associated with the display of critical attitudes. In China, for instance, 'What distinguished this tiny minority from the majority of China's intellectuals was a sense of responsibility to address issues of political policy in public forum. . . [they] regarded themselves as the conscience of society'.[7]

Of late, in countries such as Hungary and Poland the number of non-conformists has increased and those of the dedicated legitimizers have shrunk. Such changes reflect the greater official tolerance of non-conformity associated with the broad political-ideological shifts taking place in several communist states. This tolerance has also been exemplified by the semi-official Hungarian category of those 'otherwise thinking' (*maskep gondolkozok*) – a form of dissidence officially accepted as harmless. In China, 'The Party has intermittently acknowledged ideologically but certainly not legally or institutionally, that the views of intellectuals. . . may be different from those of the Party. Until that happens, it is likely that intellectuals who seek intellectual and moral autonomy will continue to do so at the price of political estrangement'.[8]

Even with such developments, the condition and number of critical versus conforming (or apolitical) intellectuals remain profoundly different in communist states from those found in the West, where most intellectuals belong to or sympathize with some sort of an adversary culture.[9] Western intellectuals, especially those in the public eye, tend almost reflexively to take an adversarial, critical position in the face of what they perceive to be the prevailing values, institutions and injustices of their society. In the West such a critical stance is compatible with secure and well paid employment (mostly provided by universities), and with opportunities to publish and otherwise disseminate publicly one's ideas.

The critical intellectuals living in communist societies contemplate with wistful longing such free expression, and especially the absence of risks associated with it and the access to secure employment and all conceivable media of communication.

Dissenting intellectuals in communist societies also differ from their Western counterparts in that they are capable (with a few exceptions) of being social critics without relying on a Marxist conceptual framework; in fact, they have no use for Marxism of any version or variety, either as a tool for social criticism and analysis or as a sustaining worldview or secular religion.[10] What Raymond Aron called 'the opium of intellectuals' in the West (and parts of the Third World) fails to animate (or narcotize) intellectuals in communist societies, including those officially engaged in the approved application, the dissemination or renovation of Marxism and Leninism. Moreover, intellectuals in these countries – again, unlike their Western counterparts – are not capable of venerating the ideals of Marxian socialism while averting their eyes from the realities of existing socialist systems which have been employing these ideals as legitimating devices and alleged guideposts for their activities in practice.

The remarks of a Hungarian dissident writer on the virtues of 'existing socialist systems' illustrate an outlook that has benefited from the attempted implementation of these theories:

'Existing'. . . . is a very broad category that can provide loop-holes for all sorts of things. It is for this reason that [Georg] Lukacs could maintain that the worst form of socialism is superior to the best form of capitalism because if socialism exists in any form then it is – from the standpoint of world history and the philosophy of history, from the standpoint of universal progress though not from that of the concrete, empirically existing individual – a higher level of development in the history of mankind. This worldview in the case of Lukacs too had its origin in the fact that the great philosopher, protecting his whole life, was reluctant to focus his great analytical powers on the question: what is it, after all, that exists? Because undoubtedly something did exist in these countries and if we chose to call it 'socialism' then in one jump we found ourselves at a higher rung of human evolution.[11]

While intellectuals in communist societies do not care much about the ideas of Marx and Lenin, they do recognize that these political systems are deeply concerned with ideas and under appropriate conditions (of compliance) allow intellectuals to occupy positions of power and influence. This state of affairs is directly linked to the major paradox in the relationship of intellectuals and communist systems, namely, that such systems take ideas seriously and treat them like weapons (which is one reason why they attract many intellectuals in the first place). Hence these states initially make good use of the support and skill of intellec-tuals (who are impressed by being taken seriously) and end up regimenting and repressing them, and depriving them of their distinctive intellectual calling, that of autonomous social critic and interpreter of ideas. Thus on the one hand Marxist-Leninist systems place great emphasis on the role of ideas, while on the other they take a highly instrumental and manipulative approach toward them. In such systems ideas are at once respected and their integrity violated time and again.

In the final analysis, then, the relationship between intel-lectuals and communist systems is determined by the fact that communist systems are both profoundly anti-intellectual and at the same time preoccupied with ideas, obsessed with finding theoretical and ideological legitimation for their policies. Such an ambivalence about the importance of ideas (and intellectuals) derives form the basic action orientation of these political systems and movements. Ideas are regarded as worthless unless they help to attain political ends and can be used in the struggle to gain and keep (and maximize) power. (Hence Lenin's contempt toward the typical Russian intellectuals perceived as unfocused talkers incapable of politically productive action; and hence his determination to build a party of professional revolutionaries of rejuvenated, newly toughened intellectuals to provide a disciplined vanguard and leadership for his policies.)[12]

The major institutional reflections of the official concern with ideas have been comprehensive censorship, the thorough refashioning of educational institutions, the monopoly over the media of mass communication and the insistence on at least overt ideological conformity on the part of the whole population.

The role of intellectuals in communist systems thus rests on the importance that these systems assign to ideas. Although, as noted above, ideas are important as tools of control, legitimation and (supposedly) guidance, the longer such systems have been in existence the less dynamic they become even as manipulators of ideas. While the vast agitprop apparatuses have shown no sign of withering away or being dismantled, the political use of ideas in communist states seems to diminish over time, and with this the part played by the functionary intellectuals.

There are at least two reasons for this development. One is the unwitting immunization of the population against official ideas and ideologies, due to the pervasive boredom and reflexive rejection they inspire over time. Another is the recognition on the part of the authorities that the compulsive regurgitation of ideas has decreasing effectiveness either as a device for inspiring and mobilizing the population or legitimating the political order which, in any event, has demonstrated its staying power if only by brute crushing of outbreaks of dissatisfaction. It also appears that not even the ruling élites find much inspiration or practical guidance in the doctrinal heritage, other than a residual assurance that they should stay in power no matter what.

Vaclav Havel's comments on this state of affairs in Czechoslovakia applies to other well-established communist systems as well:

> Seldom in recent times has a regime cared so little for the real attitudes of outwardly loyal citizens or for the sincerity of their statements. . . No one tries to convince the penitent that he was in error or acted wrongly, but simply. . . that he must repent in order to save himself. . . Think what you like in private, as long as you agree in public. . . suppress your interest in truth and silence your conscience – and the doors will be wide open to you.
>
> . . . The contrast between the revolutionary teachings about the new man and the new morality and the shoddy concept of life as consumer bliss raises the question of why the authorities actually cling so frantically to their ideology. Clearly, only because their ideology. . . assures them the appearance of legitimacy, continuity and consistency, and acts as a screen of prestige for their pragmatic practice. . .
>
> From the bowels of that infinite mountain of ideological rhetoric. . . which. . . the public, for the most part, scarcely notices, there emerges one specific and meaningful message, one realistic piece of advice: 'Avoid politics if you can; leave it to us! Just do what we tell you, don't try to have deep thoughts, and don't poke your nose into things that don't concern you! Shut up, do your work, look after yourself – and you will be all right![13]

This may well describe the communist version of 'repressive tolerance', a concept which, while never helpful for understanding the political pluralism of Western societies (where its originator, Herbert Marcuse, intended it to apply), has come to provide a measure of understanding of the policies some communist systems have followed in recent times.

The decline of the importance of official ideas and official intellectuals, while on the one hand reflecting the relative security and durability of these systems (and the degree of resigned popular acquiescence they have attained), has been accompanied by the reinvigoration of the critical intelligentsia, at least in parts of Eastern Europe, the Soviet Union and China. The intellectuals have become more vocal and influential and – born in part on the tides of glasnost – they have established a precarious quasi-legitimacy. As another Czech author put it, 'They frequently express loudly what the silenced majority actually thinks'.[14]

The influence and number of these non-conformist intellectuals vary considerably from country to country in the communist world. For example, even in less repressive Yugoslavia 'The dissident voice, although intense in Ljubljana and Belgrade, is barely audible outside these two cities, and the influence of the dissidents on the working class is still very small'.[15] By contrast, 'The terms "dissent" and "dissidents," which evoke images of a small network of isolated individuals working in an indifferent or even hostile environment seem to be particularly inadequate for describing intellectual and other opposition in Poland. A hallmark of contemporary Polish reality is the existence. . . of extensive groups and networks organized independently of the authorities. . .'[16]

Insofar as there is a ferment in communist societies, nonconformist intellectuals are in its forefront and have made it more noticeable and widely communicated. But it is also true that, as Aleksa Djilas observed, such intellectuals have little visibility and support among the working classes. Sometimes they are perceived as troublemakers not only by the authorities but also by many of their compatriots who fear change.

Could intellectuals make a substantial contribution to political change in communist systems? They could if more intellectuals of the apolitical type would join the minority of committed critics and if the functionary intellectuals would be shamed into toning down legitimating activities intended to shore up the systems. The part played by intellectuals in political change will of course also depend on their narrower political environment. In harshly repressive communist states such as those in Albania, Bulgaria, Cuba, North Korea, Vietnam, and, until recently, Bulgaria and Romania, there are few known dissenters (unless in jail) and the tradition of autonomous intellectual life itself is weak (less so in

Cuba). Thus it is obvious that broader social, political and historical conditions have much bearing on the future role and effectiveness of intellectuals in particular communist systems. Where they can engage in prolonged public criticism, their major contribution to change may be a gradual, cumulative undermining of the self-confidence and will to power of the ruling group.

At the same time, the commitment to political change on the part of intellectuals may face obstacles even under relatively favorable conditions such as those found in present day Hungary. According to Haraszti, cooptation is the danger:

> All the intellectual professions have been given political responsibilities; since everyone is a state employee, an objective bureaucratism conceals the class egotism that governs the distribution of goods and machinery of publicity. In this modernization of society the intelligentsia had nothing to lose but its independence; in return, it gained half a world, and possesses it on condition that it protect the unity of this world and interpret its own power as service.[17]

Haraszti also believes that censorship has been relaxed because 'The state need not enforce obedience when everyone has learned to police himself'.[18] Fortunately, not everyone has learned to police himself and many who learned are unlearning it; in fact, in Hungary there has been a marked decline in self-censorship. Moreover, even a marginally freer expression matters: talk is a kind of action and the more questions are raised, the more alternatives are sketched and the more cracks open in the crust of communist authoritarianism. Eventually, it becomes more difficult to legitimate the system.

While it is difficult to specify the contribution that intellectuals are currently making to the institutional transformation of communist societies, or to predict when, where and what kinds of changes will occur, a contribution of a more intangible kind is already being made along the lines suggested above in at least a few communist systems.

Moreover, harsh as it has been for non-conforming intellectuals to live under communist systems, the experience has nonetheless conferred some unforeseen and unintended blessings; if for some it has been a corrupting experience, for others it has been a purifying one . If many chose to abandon the intellectual calling by 'selling out', they did so under severe pressures. By contrast, many of their Western counterparts who in recent times have embraced assorted authoritarian movements and obscurantist ideologies, did so gratuitously and spontaneously without suffering such pressures, as a matter of poor judgment or submission to political–intellectual fads.

Thus for intellectuals under communism (or a good many of them), 'escape from freedom' and the varieties of anti-intellectualism which swept Western academic life since the 1960s have held no attraction; they have emerged free of what Kolakowski called the 'Naphta component', the search for a compelling authority outside the realm of reason and ideas. It cannot be said of them that '. . . any religious or social movement representing the most aggressive anti-intellectualism will find enthusiastic support' among them, as has been the case among 'a certain number of intellectuals brought up in Western bourgeois civilization who ostentatiously discard its values. . .' Nor will they share the 'enthusiasm of [Western] intellectuals for peasant and Lumpenproletarian movements. . .'[19]

It would be ironic if groups of intellectuals in communist societies ended up not only as the most loyal guardians of Western political values and cultural traditions but also in a better position than their Western colleagues to influence the public affairs of their societies.

In all probability, intellectuals in communist states have fewer illusions than their Western colleagues; certainly, they are freer of an oppressive sense of meaninglessness and the excesses of alienation. They are immune to the seductions of political utopias and the temptations of secular religion. In the end, they may turn out to be more capable of pursuing the attainable agenda of human improvement and liberation than their more indulged colleagues in the West.

NOTES

1. Hollander in Gagnon 1987, p. 69.
2. Churchward, 1973, pp. 128, 90, 105, 123.
3. Quoted in Churchward 1973, p. 135.
4. A typical [recent] case is that of Ariel Hidalgo, given an eight-year sentence for 'enemy propaganda' after secret police found a personal manuscript in which he assailed what he saw as a new ruling class. He was confined to a mental hospital, then jailed for a year in 'the rectangle of death', the notorious punishment wing of the Havana prison. There he spent weeks naked in a bedless cell'. (Editorial, *New York Times*, 4 August 1988.)
5. Goldman, 1981, p. 2.
6. Tismaneanu, pp. 111–12.
7. Goldman, 1981, p. 2.
8. Goldman, ed., 1987, p. 20.
9. For a detailed discussion of this concept see 'Introduction' in Hollander, 1988.
10. See *Epilogue* in Kolakowski, 1978.
11. Eorsi, 1985, p. 45.
12. Leites, 1954.
13. Havel, 1987, pp. 8–9, 14.
14. Kavan, n.d., p. 1.
15. Djilas, Aleksa, 1987, p. 8.
16. Karpinski, 1987, p. 44.
17. Haraszti, 1987, p. 18.
18. Ibid., p. 96.
19. Kolakowski, 1972, pp. 11, 12.

REFERENCES

Aczel, Tamas and Meray, Tibor (1969), *The Revolt of the Mind* (London: Thames).
Churchward, L.G. (1973), *The Soviet Intelligentsia* (London: Routledge).
Djilas, Aleksa (1987), 'Yugoslav Dissent and the Future of Communism'. Paper delivered at the Conference on *The Future of Communist States* (New York, October) (see this volume, pp. 129–34).
Djilas, Milovan (1957), *The New Class* (New York: Praeger).
Eörsi, Istvan (1985), 'Urugyeim' (My Pretexts) in *Beszelo* (an unofficial periodical in Hungary), No. 12.
Goldman, Merle (1981) *China's Intellectuals: Advise and Dissent* (Cambridge: Harvard UP).
Goldman, Merle *et al.* (ed)(1987), *China's Intellectuals and the State, In Search of a New Relationship* (Cambridge: Harvard UP).
Haraszti, Miklós (1987), *The Velvet Prison – Artists Under State Socialism* (New York: Basic Books).

Havel, Vaclav (1987), 'Letter to Dr. Gustav Husak' in Vladislav, J. (ed.) *Vaclav Havel, or Living in Truth* (London: Faber).

Hollander, Paul (1981, 1983), *Political Pilgrims* (New York: Oxford UP; Harper & Row).

Hollander, Paul (1987), 'American Intellectuals: Producers and Consumers of Social Criticism' in Alain G. Gagnon (ed.), *Intellectuals in Liberal Democracies* (New York: Prager).

Hollander, Paul (1988), *The Survival of the Adversary Culture* (New Brunswick: Transaction).

Karpinski, Jakub (1987), 'Polish Intellectuals in Opposition', *Problems of Communism*, July–August.

Kavan, Jan (no date), 'Charter 77 in dialogue with other independent movements' (London: Palach Press, newsletter).

Kolakowski, Leszek (1972), 'Intellectuals Against Intellect' *Daedalus*, Summer, No. 3.

Kolakowski, Leszek (1978), 'Epilogue' in *Main Currents of Marxism* (New York: Oxford UP), Vol. III.

Konrád, George and Szelenyi, Ivan (1979), *The Intellectuals on the Road to Class Power* (New York: Harcourt).

Leites, Nathan (1954), *A Study of Bolshevism* (Glencoe: Free Press).

Markov, Georgi (1984) *The Truth that Killed* (New York: Ticknore).

Milosz, Czeslaw, (1955), *The Captive Mind* (New York: Vintage).

Ripoll, Carlos (1985), 'Harnessing the Intellectual: Censoring Writers and Artists in Today's Cuba' (Washington: Cuban American National Foundation).

Ripoll, Carlos (1986), 'The Crisis of Culture in Cuba' (University of Miami: Institute of Interamerican Studies).

Tismaneanu, Vladimir (1988), *The Crisis of Marxist Ideology in Eastern Europe: The Poverty of Utopia* (London and New York: Routledge).

20 East Bloc Intellectuals
Antonin Liehm

What exactly is the situation and role of intellectuals and culture in socialist countries? Are they court jesters, peddlers of ideology, high priests and creators of myths, builders of monuments, official painters and portraitists? Or are they the eternal martyrs of totalitarianism, victims of its institutionalized censorships, keepers of the flame of dissent, Cassandras to whom nobody listens, witnesses who eventually testify before the world to all crimes and arbitrariness?

They are both of these, depending upon where you look.

The two roles sketched above are simplified extremes. The problem is that the general public easily comes to the conclusion that such demonstrative simplifications stand for reality. Many people all over the world imagine that Russia or Russian totalitarianism equals the KGB on one side and the dissidents or refuseniks on the other; they forget, or never even think of the 250 million Soviet citizens who find themselves between the two.

If the situation were that simple, then Gorbachev's role and task – and for that matter, to some degree that of any leader in Eastern Europe – would be easy. It would be sufficient for a reformist leader to have the support of the KGB and to give legal status to the dissidents; together they would all dance forward on the bright highway of progress. The problem, among others, is that although a secretary general of the Soviet communist party could easily bring the late Sakharov back from Gorky and allow him to appear on foreign television and dine with foreign prime ministers, nobody in Russia knows who Sakharov was, and what is more, nobody cares.

Thus the basic situation of intellectuals in the USSR and Central Europe is not very different from that of their peers in other European societies throughout the centuries. Intellectuals, creators of art and culture, are a strange breed who by definition are a nuisance not only to those in power but also to the general population – disliked in periods of calm and prosperity, adorned in periods of turbulence, scorned or at best ignored in periods of defeat and disaster. It is no surprise that the only affluent democratic modern society whose history has been an almost uninterrupted success story profoundly dislikes its eggheads and on the whole ignores them.

Intellectuals have always been the spokesman of human and social malaise. Their authority grows and fades with the progress and decline of one malaise after another. For centuries in Europe they used varying means of expression, ranging from the Socratic and Dionysiac ones to carnivals, religious heresies and anti-authoritarian attitudes. They usually paid according to the customs of the society and the times. Neither ideological or social change, nor fundamental reform, including of course revolutions, are imaginable without intellectuals and the ideas, impulses and participation they provide. However, no successful reform or revolution has much use for intellectuals and soon it drives them into the opposition, chastising them accordingly, to the near indifference of the millions who only yesterday followed or applauded them. Although I am not writing a manifesto about the fundamental nature of the situation of intellectuals in the totalitarian European societies of today and the European societies of yesterday, there are historical parallels which we must understand to be able to grasp what is happening now.

Both the Russian revolutions would have been unimaginable without the Russian intellectuals and artists who played a tremendous role in the dismantling of the ideological structure of pre-revolutionary society. In the countries of East Central Europe, beginning with the GDR and ending with Bulgaria, intellectuals, as prophets or fellow travelers, often prepared the way for the imposition or acceptance of the Soviet model. In both cases the vast majority of them perished, physically or morally, in the victorious cataclysm. But their peers were to be found almost immediately within the new structures, new Cassandras expressing the new malaise, the hopes betrayed, the trust and honesty denied. Once again they paid, as the promoters and heroes of the next era became its targets and ultimately its victims.

This is a pattern, which in some ways exists everywhere, with specific differences tied to each country's history, tradition, memory and situation. Today as much as yesterday, one example of these differences is that in Russia nationalism is a philosophy of conservation and in the non-Russian countries it is a philosophy of change.

How does all this apply to the present situation in the USSR and European socialist countries?

In the USSR, the latest intellectual malaise began after the overthrow of Khrushchev. It led not only to more or less open dissent but also to multiple complex internal struggles which have already been much discussed. It is, however, only now that we see what was really happening. Look at those sometimes astonishing Soviet films now being released after years on the shelves. They were all made during the most difficult years and passed all of the obstacles but the last – distribution. Now all of this is coming out into the open. Gorbachev needs intellectuals and creators to help him get his message across, and at the same time he is asking them not to overstep the boundaries. But where do these frontiers lie? Not even the Politburo seems to agree, and the differences grow the further away from it you get. There is, however, an even bigger problem: the intellectuals, artists and creative thinkers necessarily must overstep the boundaries, for this is the essence of their existence. The more Russia moves toward increasing openness, the less dramatic this will be: the stronger the resistance, the more dramatic and even tragic the role of the intellectuals will become.

Outside of the USSR, the three countries in which intellectuals and culture in general will again play an important role are obviously Poland, Czechoslovakia and Hungary. But it will not just be the repetition of that which has already been experienced. In Poland the society is becoming tired and more apathetic than ever before during the last 40 years. Paradoxically, while the unofficial parallel culture is still growing and while Poland remains today probably the freest of the socialist countries concerning freedom of expression, the influence of the intellectuals and the cultural strata is diminishing.

In Hungary – in this respect not as free as Poland – the intellectual impetus has been to a large extent absorbed by changes in the economic structure. If this should continue successfully, cultural production will soon be feeling the pressures of even a limited market economy and intellectuals will start playing more and more the role of Cassandra, as they did during the most difficult years of Stalinism or the post-1956 period, though of course for different reasons.

In Czechoslovakia, where, for historical reasons, the participation of intellectuals in the political life of the country was the strongest, much was done during the past 20 years to suppress their traditions, influence and creativity. This Inquisition was to a large degree successful. We can now feel a slow awakening from a long stupor and can even see the beginning of a differentiation within the official intellectual and cultural establishment. We can probably expect a progressive narrowing of the gap between the official and unofficial cultures and the lifting of some bans, but nothing analogous to that which took place in the 1960s is in sight at this point. [This assessment reflects the stalemate in Czechoslovakian society during the last years of the Husák regime. (Eds)]

There are, of course, two important differences between the USSR and the majority of the socialist countries. Unlike in Russia, in the other countries there exists what could be called a democratic reflex, a liberal subconscious, a long experience of freedom and of a fight for it along lines known in other parts of Europe. Forty often turbulent years during which this spirit could have been wiped out have proved insufficient. In the other socialist countries, everybody knows who Sakharov was, and a great many people in addition to those within the cultural and intellectual strata still care. Much less is needed than in Russia for the democratic reflex to begin and for this liberal subconscious to reach the surface.

The other difference is nationalism. As a superpower, the Soviet Union knows a new kind of nationalism that coincides with Russian national pride. It is hard to believe that this kind of Soviet nationalism does not exist even in the non-Russian areas where local, anti-Russian nationalism clearly prevails. Obviously, there is a conflict that will come to the surface during the process of reform. In the other socialist countries, the situation is much clearer: any nationalism has acquired an anti-Soviet, anti-Russian connotation. This is true even in a country like Czechoslovakia, where it never existed, and in Bulgaria, where it was considered unthinkable. Everyone feels that the USSR is the cause of their troubles and problems, and even an appeal to national pride takes on dangerous connotations. Unlike in the USSR, this can also almost immediately trigger an outburst which usually has the intellectuals and the cultural sphere at its center.

To conclude, the more affluent, open, democratic and liberal a European society, the less important is the political role played by intellectuals and culture. Their role grows in inverse proportion to the shrinking of the space within which they can operate freely, coinciding with the limitation of everyone's freedom and independence. Intellectuals and culture are bound to play an important social and political role in authoritarian and totalitarian societies. This role will diminish only if these societies reach a greater degree of internal balance between those who govern and those governed, giving the latter at least some access to greater affluence. We know that intellectuals and creators of culture do not seek their special and extremely uncomfortable position; they are driven into it and try to leave it as soon as some degree of political process has been restored, as the Czech and Polish examples illustrate. In the meantime, their testimony, based on an experience new to European humanity, helps us to discover new facets of human experience. This has been proven by the sometimes extraordinary international success of their literary and polemical work.

21 A View From Bucharest
Mihai Botez

As a Romanian mathematician and futurist, I have had the privilege to see 'from within' how intellectuals and the communist state can coexist in Eastern Europe. In my experience, East European intellectuals do not represent a threat to existing communist rule, although they can challenge it. [Few people – if any at all – could have foreseen the amplitude of the anti-communist upheaval in Romania in December 1989. At the same time, some of the predictions made in this paper retain their validity even after the breakdown of the Ceausescu regime. The new ruling body – the National Salvation Front – is overwhelmingly made up of former communists. Their strategy is to preserve some institutions of the old order by changing their names but not their functions. In the meantime, opposition parties have emerged in Romania and the transition to post-communism has proceeded faster than expected. (Eds)]

If 'intellectuals' means, in the broad sense, 'better-educated people who earn their living from mental rather than manual labor' (and therefore including routine white-collar employees as well as the creative and critical intelligentsia), then what could 'East European intellectuals' mean? Are intellectuals living in Eastern Europe a new species of intellectual?

Further, if a State is, in Max Weber's definition, 'an organization which can successfully claim the monopoly of the legitimate use of physical force within a given territory', and therefore a communist state is a state in which 'physical force' is in the hands of the sole ruling Marxist party, then what could a 'National-Communist State' mean? Is such an organization a new one?

My conviction is that both these categories are now realities, and that Romanian intellectuals, as well as the Romanian communist state, fully illustrate them. For me, as a futurist, the present is not only the result and final stage of the past; it is also the starting point for the future. I will not, therefore, describe the past wars, with their victories and defeats, between intellectuals and communist power; I will only try to discover, in the present situations, the seeds of possible future developments.

EAST-EUROPEAN INTELLECTUALS: ARE THEY REALLY A NEW SPECIES OF INTELLECTUAL?

Intellectuals belong to 'civil society'. Usually analyses of the relationships between Soviet-type regimes and 'civil society' are at two extremes.

At one extreme we find those analyses which assume a total divorce between the society and the communist power: essentially hostile to human nature, they claim, the totalitarian system was introduced by force (first in the USSR, to be further exported, by force also, to other communist countries), and the repressed society has no other wish but to get rid of it and to resume the course of its natural (that is democratic) development. Representations of this sort are frequent in writings of dissenting authors like Aleksandr Solzhenitsyn or Paul Goma.

At the other extreme we find analyses which argue that societies in communist countries have been totally pervaded by the Soviet-type system. A symbiosis has occurred, leading to genuine communization. Ironically, here Zinoviev's sarcasm converges with the eulogies of official communist authors. The endurance of the Soviet-type system no longer appears to be based on fear but on the total assimilation and natural integration of the new structure – in the USSR and other communist countries alike. In short, communism is perceived as a genetic mutation.

My personal view is in between. It would be hard to believe that decades of communist rule and imposed-by-force behavior have passed without any consequence; but adaptation for survival is a sign of health and vigor. Thus some tenets of communism, and some patterns of behavior under dictatorship, have probably been internalized. But this does not mean that once freed from dictatorship the citizen produced by and for totalitarian society will perform like a Westerner produced by and for democracy. Therefore, it is difficult to say what 'health' means, if once cured the patient is not behaving like a 'normal' human being – normal being here understood 'according to Western standards'. In short, I perceive communism as an incurable illness, with some genetic effects on an immature body – like polio in childhood.

Intellectuals living in communist countries are infected by this illness like all other citizens of those countries. But their sickness has some additional features. As 'products' of a communist regime, their intellectual formation is often imprinted by communist ideology and official culture. (Obviously, these things affect technocrats less than 'culturecrats' – if I may so call the non-technocratic intelligentsia, such as humanists and artists.) As 'producers' for a communist regime, their behavior is also influenced by the totalitarian rules of the one-party-controlled society: for instance, they have little understanding of the intellectual market.

Communist power, at least in its first period of domination, was anti- or a-intellectual. According to the classic blue-collar approach, intellectuals do not form a social class and even less a ruling class. Therefore, their access to real power is limited and they are condemned to remain second-order members of the new society. Let us also recall the latent hostility of the early communist leaders toward the only owners of a means of production that cannot be nationalized by force: *intellectual brilliance is personal, and cannot be transferred by simple decrees.* Finally, at least in Eastern Europe, many intellectuals came from old bourgeois classes. They were perceived as enemies by the new rulers, and this hostility was transferred to the whole social group.

Modern communist society has partly modified this classic approach. Neo-Marxist analyses argue that in the age of scientific–technological and media revolutions, both technocrats and culturecrats, masters of these new means of production, should be included in the new, extended, ruling 'working class'. But the feeling of marginalization and frustration is still widespread among intellectuals of the communist countries.

In addition, East European intellectuals are facing the general difficulties of belonging to a small culture: with the exception of the Russians (and perhaps the Germans), they feel that the role of their cultures in international dialogue is marginal, and that they themselves are often perceived as exotic products of peripheral areas. An inferiority/superiority complex has thus emerged.

All these special conditions have created a new species of intellectual: the East/European intellectual. In the field of intellectual creation, the specificity is not very visible. Geniuses and mediocrities coexist as everywhere else. But the societal behavior of such intellectuals (and possibly their intellectual behavior) would be perceived as peculiar by Western colleagues. Few Western intellectuals, for instance, could understand what 'internal exile' means, and probably fewer could share the difficulties of an exiled East European intellectual.

THE NATIONAL-COMMUNIST STATE: AN EMERGING REALITY

In contrast to Russia, where the communist order resulted from the internal conflicts of the tsarist empire, the introduction of the Soviet-type system in Eastern Europe cannot be separated from the impact of external factors, such as the victorious march of the Red Army to Berlin (1944–45) and the political and military balance of forces prevailing in postwar Europe.

Western views on Eastern Europe have changed during the past four decades. In the 1950s, the area was considered a docile family of quasi-identical Soviet satellites. By contrast, in the 1970s, partly due to the US policy of 'differentiation', many analysts speaking of the Romanian or Polish leaders seemed to have forgotten that they were also (if not primarily) communists, just like the leaders of the Kremlin. The prevalent image of the area was that of a collection of Western-like nation-states languishing under Soviet military domination and hardly able to wait for an opportunity to liberate themselves; the corollary of this approach is that once Soviet domination is ended, the Soviet-type systems in the other countries will vanish, since theirs cannot survive without 'big brother' sponsorship.

My own view is that while it is unquestionable that the totalitarian Stalinist seeds produced various fruits on the varying soils of East European national traditions, nevertheless, all these fruits belong to the same species – namely, the communist state. That communism is more visible in Romania than, say, in Hungary doesn't mean that these two countries are structurally different: the difference is between a primitive and an evolved communist dictatorship.

What could national-communism thus mean?

It has been said many times that nationalism and communism offer opposite views of the world: one sees a set of different, interacting nations; another sees two interacting social classes which transcend national boundaries. Thus national-communism seems to be a contradiction in terms. In addition, nationalism has right-wing political connotations, while communism has left-wing ones. In practical terms, in the late 1940s and early 1950s in East Europe, 'love for the USSR' was perceived as internationalism, while all other nationalisms were branded reactionary and condemned. If we recall the role of the Soviet factor in the establishment of Soviet-type regimes in the area, it is obvious why so many East Europeans have associated 'Soviet' with 'communism' and 'nationalism' with 'anti-Sovietism' and 'anti-communism'. This seems to offer new arguments for the logical incompatibility of nationalism and communism, at least beyond the USSR.

All this notwithstanding, a new reality emerges in Eastern Europe: the strange marriage between nationalism and communism, whose result is national-communism. But why would nationalism be attracted by communism?

Many sociologists offer competent explanations for the rise of nationalism and even chauvinism and xenophobia in our modern transnational world; in this respect, Eastern Europe is not different from other areas. In addition, the nationalist myth remains one of the few myths that has resisted contemporary iconoclastic criticism – and also benefited from the failure of other myths, like that of the communist utopia of social equity. One should also note the role of nationalism in small, marginal nations like the majority of East European nations, which have historically felt threatened by empires and superpowers.

After 40 years of communist rule, and so many unsuccessful challenges to this rule, many people in Eastern Europe share the conviction that there is no realistic alternative to the

communist regime in the area. [The extraordinary changes
that took place in the region in 1989 have shown that this resignation to the status quo is less pervasive and paralysing than
many scholars and civic rights activists would have thought.
(Eds)] It is also to be noted that the imperfect democratic
regimes of the pre-war period have become too distant in
the past to sustain their impact on the new societies. In
addition, the Western-democratic experience is little known,
and for many people appears irrelevant to the real conditions
of our area.

Therefore, a common feeling is that the only possible
patriotic involvement includes acceptance of the dominant
communist rule. If the only realistic version of Romania
or Bulgaria is the communist one, then to accept the communist social contract becomes synonymous with accepting
one's national heritage; to deny it means abandoning one's
traditional background and condemning oneself to internal
or external exile.

This may explain why nationalists in Eastern Europe can
be attracted by communism, but why are communist élites
attracted by nationalism?

First, after 40 years of domination, such élites have usually
created their own national instruments for preserving power
(a powerful party apparatus, political police, censorship, and
so on) and are now able to govern without manifest Soviet
support.

Second, perceived for years as Soviet puppets, these regimes
can find in their emphasis on nationalist feelings and traditions the internal and external legitimacy any unelected
government seeks.

Third, the masses' nationalistic feelings can be manipulated
to achieve communist goals, establishing some resonance or
even a genuine alliance between rulers and ruled that otherwise would be unthinkable.

National-communism appears more attractive than nationalism or communism taken separately; together they seem
diluted, less ideological and more pragmatic, and therefore
humanized. No longer viewed as Moscow-guided, no longer
associated with Soviet hegemony (and therefore no longer
perceived as a threat by the West) no longer responsible for
past crimes and mistakes (explained away by the perfidious

'external factor'), enjoying the benefits of any 'new beginning', such a new form of communism could look quite appealing to rulers, ruled and foreigners, too.

At the same time, pure nationalism or chauvinism/xenophobia can appear less dangerous when married to a traditionally transnational ideology like communism.

Let us pass now over the first historical success of national-communism, the Soviet mobilization of the masses during World War II on behalf of 'Mother Russia', to Romania, the first contemporary successful experience of national-communism in Europe. In that country, orthodox communism and sharp nationalism strengthened each other and also strengthened the existing supreme-type leadership. The old adage changed: 'whoever is now with us communists is against us', became 'whoever does not cheer the national-communist president is against his own country'.

It has been said that Romania is an exceptional case: primitive communism and primitive nationalism feed each other to create left-wing and right-wing dictatorships within the same totalitarian structure.[The Romanian revolution, with its violence and martyrs, demonstrated how deeply entrenched the terrorist procedures had been under Ceausescu. At the same time, the heroic uprising of the population showed the limits of any totalitarian system. (Eds)]

Under the impact of the 'Gorbachev effect', new centripetal nationalisms will probably emerge in the near future both within and beyond the USSR, especially in Eastern Europe. The natural consequence will be the emergence of national-communist states. It is also plausible that these states will inherit the historically--unsolved traditional 'national problems'. *A period of latent and/or open conflicts among national-communist states of Eastern Europe is thus to be expected.*

EAST-EUROPEAN INTELLECTUALS AND THE NATIONAL-COMMUNIST STATE: A MORE APPEALING SOCIAL CONTRACT?

No political system is either fully supported or totally rejected by the population, and communism and intellectuals are no exception to this general situation. In addition, intellectuals and any power are often in conflict. However, the relationships between intellectuals and communist power are special. It has been said many times that 'intellectual' means freedom – of thinking without taboos, of expression without *a priori* constraints, of travel without borders, and so on; criticism is also a genuine characteristic of intellectual awareness. The expression 'critical intellectual' is often perceived as a tautology, for intellectuals are by definition critical. But communist power means totalitarianism and therefore explicit taboos (such as criticizing Marxist ideology or the one-party system). Intellectuals and communism seem logically incompatible.

However, it would be foolish to claim that in the communist world there are no intellectuals: Soviet music, Polish mathematics or Romanian poetry prove the contrary.

This means that many intellectuals have accepted the invisible social contract of the Soviet-type regime. This contract is more painful for intellectuals than for other people. 'Living within the Lie', as Havel would say, can become impossible. History shows that intellectuals have been the principal source of criticism of the regime (as in the USSR, GDR, Czechoslovakia and Romania), and if by 'dissident' we understand, with Roy Medvedev, 'someone who disagrees. . . with the ideological, political, economic, or moral foundation that every society rests on. . . openly proclaiming his dissent and demonstrating it. . . to his compatriots and the State', then generally speaking the dissidents in the communist world come from the intelligentsia. In addition, intellectuals have played major roles in many incidents of 'mass unrest'; it suffices to remember the history of KOR and Solidarnosc in Poland.

Sometimes one argues that intellectuals living under communist rule face the terrible choice between being courtiers or dissidents – or, as Kolakowski put it, 'priests or jesters'. However, in my view to accept the communist social contract does not mean it is obligatory to become a courtier – and many East European technocrats can prove that. There exists also a true 'art of survival' under dictatorship – combining well-calculated submission, self-limited criticism, tactical keeping of a 'low profile' and use of opportunities. For Western intellectuals, such 'strategies' frequently seem strange, if not disgusting. I can only express my hope that nobody will force them in the future to learn such an art.

All these remarks concern the relationships between intellectuals and the 'standard' communist state. What does national-communism introduce that is new within this scheme? Especially in Eastern Europe, the national-communist state proposes to intellectuals a more appealing social contract than the standard communist one. In the frame of a national-communist regime, honest intellectuals may find communism distasteful but will be committed to national values and prestige: thus, for patriotic reasons they will not reject the 'communist social contract'. For intellectuals from small or medium-sized countries, such reasons can play an important role.

Let us imagine a cost-benefit analysis of the alternatives that the East European intellectual is facing: positive support, positive acceptance, negative acceptance and active rejection of the national-communist social contract. The moral cost of support and acceptance is lower in this case than in a standard communist regime: decent intellectuals often persuade themselves that patriotic feelings motivate their active or passive cooperation with power. The benefits of positive support are obvious: promotion and professional/social achievement. The benefits of positive acceptance include normal national professional life and permission to participate in international professional life. Negative acceptance usually means that access to the international arena is not guaranteed. As for the active rejection of the social contract, the result is clear: internal or external exile.

Obviously, this scheme is oversimplified. Sociologists who are studying the different forms of 'second society' emerging now in Hungary, Poland or Czechoslovakia will probably argue that the social contract can be only formally and partially accepted. That is true. And even the sad experience of Romania, where the 'second society' is not parallel as it is in Poland or Hungary, but mixed up and entangled in the texture of the visible one, substantiates the difficulties of such elementary taxomony. But it is also true that decision-makers frequently place intellectuals in the above-mentioned boxes, and that their behavior, and its consequences for the ruled, is guided by such oversimplifications.

The support-acceptance of the national-communist social contract seems natural for a technocrat: if fortunate, our subject can also benefit from the internationalization of intellectual life, which has been so politicized in the last decades. In fact, it is chic to have natives from exotic areas such as Eastern Europe in international professional organizations. Once allowed to perform on the international stage, our subject can transform this into an extremely fruitful experience.

However, the rejection of the national-communist contract is less painful for a technocrat than for a culturecrat: internal/external exile is generally supportable, and does not imply obligatory professional silence. By contrast, for a culturecrat – and especially for someone produced by and for a small, marginalized culture – internal/external exile means silence and professional suicide.

The acceptance of the national-communist social contract now appears merely normal. If we add the patriotic motivations so important for frustrated intellectuals of marginal areas, we will no longer be surprised by the fact that in Eastern Europe the number of 'dissident culturecrats' is relatively small in comparison with that of 'consent culturecrats'.

In conclusion, the intellectuals of Eastern Europe appear tempted to accept the national-communist contract more willingly than were their predecessors, or at least not to reject it as actively. That appears rational not only from an opportunistic perspective but also in consideration of the patriotic motivations that now play such an essential role in strengthening the communist system in Europe. [Again, this diagnosis describes the pre-revolutionary situation in Eastern Europe. After 1989, is is obvious, many interpretations have had to undergo significant, even fundamental, revision. (Eds)]

Old and new national hostilities are to be expected in Eastern Europe in the near future. It is plausible to expect that national-communist governments and élites will try to use these conflicts, mobilizing people against (always foreign) enemies. In such conditions of national wars, when national identity appears to be in danger due to the 'perfidy' of neighbors, to accept the national contract (even in its communist form) becomes a patriotic duty. 'Social criticism' and dissent will look like second-order futilities in comparison to commitment to national heritage and values. As a result, national-communist states will be strengthened. In addition, national-communist states will be tacitly accepted on the world stage simply as nation-states: the old dream of introducing communism into the national option, to be accepted as an unavoidable adjective, will then come true.

In Romania, we experienced this situation some years ago. Many decent intellectuals cheered and joined the patriotic and xenophobic leadership, motivated by nationalist commitment. They adopted the government's views and campaigned in some nationalistic wars against other intellectuals. Their prestige strengthened and even legitimized the communist leadership. But once in the army, they were treated like soldiers. And many of them are now facing the painful situation of belonging to an army which, now following communist rather than nationalist goals, destroys our own historic and cultural heritage.

TOWARDS A MORE BALANCED SOCIAL CONTRACT: AUTONOMOUS UNITED INTELLECTUALS VERSUS NATIONAL-COMMUNIST STATES

Addressing the Madrid Conference on European Cultural Space in 1985, I tried to point out the imbalance of the existing social contract between intellectuals and communist power and also suggested some strategies for a more balanced contract. First, it is to be noted that the intellectuals are, directly or indirectly, state employees – the communist state is the only legal employer of intellectual work. Therefore, an essential condition for a renegotiation of a more balanced social contract is increased autonomy and even liberation of intellectuals from their patrons. I advocate the selective use of Western opportunities for endowment of autonomy of 'critical intellectuals' living under communist rule.

Another element should be added to this strategy: the selective use of our Eastern opportunities to reach the same goals. That becomes really important if we are also taking into account the danger of nationalization – and then atomization – of Eastern European critical intellectuals, as we have seen in the previous section.

This is not an easy task. Theoretically, critical intellectuals repressed in their own countries can be backed by their more fortunate colleagues from other communist countries (for example, translated, published, sponsored, and so on). The tools of liberation such as samizdat, the underground press, can also be used by critical intellectuals from abroad, favoring the development of solidarity not only within the ruled class of a nation, but also among the united ruled classes of the communist system. In practice, however, such strategies face major obstacles such as the unbalanced development of the 'second society' in different communist countries and the difficulties of communication.

It would thus seem unfair for intellectuals from some countries to benefit from such an alliance without the realistic possibility of compensation for those less fortunate, such as the Romanians.

In addition, some disturbing nationalistic ingredients are visible in the community of East European critical intellectuals. When the Dissident Joint Communiqué on the 30th anniversary of the Hungarian Revolution was made public, Romanians and Bulgarians were simply ignored, apparently for historical reasons: in those countries, 'mass unrest' against communist rule was unknown. But the price paid by the Romanian people in the 1950s is probably comparable with the price paid by other Central European countries in the same period, and for Bulgaria the situation is similar. Furthermore, I am ill at ease with a logic which asserts that if something has not happened, it will never happen.

Special efforts are thus necessary to unify East European critical intellectuals. Let us resist nationalist-diversionist propaganda: we should always remember and recall who is our first, common adversary. Also, let us analyze ourselves: our countries' past and present, as well as our own behavior, are excellent subjects for critical exercises. Such self-criticism can develop new sources of intellectual cooperation and understanding. Finally, positive actions are necessary in order to promote the union of critical intellectuals. Our alliance can transform us into a pressure group *vis-à-vis* totalitarian power. Our possible successes can also attract intellectuals from the silent majority to join our ranks. Let us imagine the enormous power of a growing group acting under the slogan. 'Critical intellectuals of all lands, unite!'

22 The Anguish and Joy of the Polish Intellectual

Aleksander Smolar

To appreciate the position of Polish intellectuals today, it would be useful to recall the beginning of the 1960s, when Khrushchev introduced important changes in the Soviet Union and there was optimism for the future of communist countries. When Khrushchev told the West that 'we will bury you', he didn't mean military destruction but the inevitable superiority of a communist organization which assured a higher lever of rationality in collective action, economic progress and social justice. Even if intellectuals were not mentioned in this context, their major role was obvious. This was no longer a time for revolutionaries but for rational, scientific planning for future development. Knowledge, rather than fidelity or ideological devotion, officially became the highest virtue.

In Western analyses, which at the time were very much influenced by the concept of convergence of socialism and capitalism, intellectuals also played a crucial role. Many studies stressed the inevitable meritocratic transformation of communist societies, the integration of intellectuals into the ruling élite, their cooptation and so on.

Quite similar hypotheses were formulated in the communist countries by official sociologists, and, without enthusiasm, by some critics on the Left, who had already seen, as in the title of a book by György Konrád and Ivan Selenyi, 'intellectuals on the road to class power'.

Today the picture is quite different. Nobody speaks about the power of intellectuals. The intellectual capacity of the power élite is probably greater than it was a quarter of a century ago, at least in Poland. But more intelligent power does not mean that intellectuals are in power. They are more remote from real sources of power than they were in Khrushchev's time. Although this is the case in all countries of the Soviet bloc, nowhere has the divorce between intellectuals and communist power been so radical as in Poland.

The role of intellectuals in Poland today is the result of a particular history and social structure. In the partitioned Poland of the nineteenth century, intellectuals played the role of state leaders. By necessity, a 'government of souls' replaced the non-existent national government. The role of the intellectuals was also the result of economic underdevelopment: civil society was epitomized not by a successful bourgeoisie but by intellectuals, in most cases of noble origin.

Their tradition and position transformed the intellectual élite into an élite not only of knowledge, verbal creativity and artistic imagination, but also into a political and social élite. To be part of this élite was not only a privilege but also a duty, which carried with it a moral obligation to serve and lead the nation. The Polish romantic poets of the nineteenth century were the archetypes of these Polish intellectuals.

After World War II the overwhelming majority of Polish intellectuals betrayed this historic national mission. They abandoned their critical role and acknowledged the superiority of the 'collective intellectual' – to use Gramsci's term – and the communist party as the new embodiment of their old virtues.

Why did this occur? This subject is extensively discussed in Polish independent publications. There are two fundamental interpretations. The first explains the intellectuals' fall as a result of cowardice, opportunism and greed. The second – put forward by those who recall their own distant past – stresses their apocalyptic feelings after the horrors of World War II, the sense that the collapse of the old world was irreversible and not to be lamented, their alienation from a society which they saw as dominated by traditional nationalism and xenophobia and their estrangement from the Catholic Church, which was identified with an obscurantist, nationalist, anti-liberal tradition. They also remember their hopes for the modernization of their underdeveloped country, for reforms rendering the country more just, for Enlightenment – even if imposed by barbarian means.

The divorce between communist power and the intellectuals developed in 1954–56 and was practically complete by the end of the 1960s. Although a similar pattern can be observed in other communist countries, the final rupture was more definitive and dramatic in Poland than elsewhere: the 'March events' (1968) ended the process. Polish intellectuals usually stress – for understandable reasons – their progressive detachment from communism, but equally important was the change of the party's attitude. The communist parties of the 1960s were no longer revolutionary vanguards looking for a radical transformation of society. They no longer needed intellectuals as the 'engineers of souls'. Nor did they need them to confirm the party's claim to cognitive, moral and prophetic legitimacy as the leader of society. Rather, they needed specialist enforcers of pragmatically-defined objectives.

The situation of the intellectuals in the 1960s was thus ambiguous. They became progressively more independent intellectually and politically. Hopes for a transformation of communism into a democratic system rapidly disappeared. But the intellectuals did not identify themselves with the society at large, which they still regarded as anti-democratic, xenophobic, clerical and threatening. The concept of two enemies – communist power and the Catholic Church – seemed to dominate the most influential intellectual circles. Patriotic feelings or attachment to tradition were seen as suspect manifestations of traditional nationalism. Isolated and alienated, the Polish intellectual was profoundly unhappy. He was truly the 'free floating' intellectual described by Karl Mannheim. It is not surprising, therefore, that this was a period of true spiritual communion between Polish and Western intellectuals, most of whom were, of course, leftist. They lived in the same spiritual universe: they shared the same values, fears and hopes and they felt equally lonely.

The turning point came in the 1970s, with the emergence of the democratic opposition and the reconstitution of a united intellectual class. For the first time, ex-communists, fellow travelers, Catholic intellectuals, liberals, nationalists and conservatives – those who served power and those who refused to do so – thought alike and acted jointly. Their common objectives were expressed in the clearest and most effective way by the KOR (Committee of Workers' Defense) movement: the defense of fundamental values and human rights, the reconstruction of a civil society outside the state and, if necessary, in opposition to it. Following the Stalinist experience, the humble Polish intellectual no longer aspired to lead the nation, give the lesson and judge the people; he wanted to serve. He refused the ambiguities of politics but his attitude was not apolitical: it was anti-political. The objective of the democratic opposition was to limit communist power and the social, economic and cultural space occupied by it, and in this way partially to liberate society.

The intellectual opposition largely contributed to the emergence of Solidarity ('the workers' revolution with a holy cross and against Marxism' – Leszek Kolakowski). For Polish intellectuals, it was a glorious moment of rehabilitation and purification. The movement they had dreamed about appeared: it was pure, generous, democratic and non-violent, and it was born with their help.

Paradoxically, however, this was also for intellectuals the moment of the second fall. This time it was not a moral one: after their demotion by communist power at the beginning of its rule, they were now dethroned by the new worker élite. The names of the new national heroes and leaders were unknown only a day before: Walesa, Walentynowicz, Bujak, Frasyniuk. Although intellectuals played an important role in the movement, they were deprived of legitimacy. They were accepted as advisors and counsellors, but not as leaders of the nation. Of course, participating actively in collective advancement, most of them felt little bitterness at their loss of power.

Ironically, one could see a moment of glorious comeback for intellectuals following the proclamation of Martial Law on 13 December 1981. When a brutal military operation destroyed the legal Solidarity movement, the majority, materially degraded and politically humiliated, went back to its usual silent condition. They did not forget the 16 months of freedom, but they were busy with everyday hardships and skeptical about the possibility of change.

A minority, however, numerous as never before, refused to abandon public space. It was no longer a time for deeds; it was a time for words. The possibility of practical action was extremely limited, but the universe of the word – the natural sphere of the intellectual – remained large despite repressions. This was the time for a symbolic politics, a politics of gesture, a politics of testifying to moral integrity, all of which are the intellectual's traditional means of public expression.

The resistance of intellectuals, writers and artists (including television boycotts by actors, boycotts of the official press by writers and journalists, and so on) had become the symbol of national resistance. The intellectuals contributed greatly to the creation of the underground independent press and publishing houses; they gave lectures in private homes and in churches, and organized private theatrical spectacles and painting exhibitions; they still play an important role in the Solidarity and non-Solidarity underground. They also play an important role in above-ground, legal and not-so-legal independent activities.

The Polish intellectual is now happy. This is not, of course, because martial law was imposed – in this respect, he shares the feelings of the general population. But he is happy in spite of the general disaster because he no longer has moral problems. He is, as the well-known essayist Andrzej Kijowski has written, finally at home: at home in his nation, at home in the Church. He is reconciled with the people, with himself, with his perception of his own historical role. He is no longer alone.

However, the period of happiness may soon be over. The Polish intellectual is frustrated. First, he hasn't really regained his social and historical role, for there is another 'collective intellectual' who has greater claims to spiritual power: the Catholic Church. Strong as never before, the Church has admirably passed a difficult test under communist rule. It is no longer predominantly plebeian and does not limit itself to pastoral work. It has developed various lay activities aimed at different groups such as workers, peasants, students, scouts and intellectuals, and serves as protector of the new forms of autonomy. But the Church has not only become the living space for a variety of public and cultural activities; it is playing a more and more openly political role. Furthermore, this political function is tacitly recognized by the communist authorities, for two reasons: they are too weak to refuse the Church a share of *de facto* power; and rather than look for a *modus vivendi* with the opposition they find it preferable to deal with the predictable and realistic approach of an institution with a long tradition of adapting to difficult conditions.

The Polish intellectual thus finds himself in an uncomfortable position between the communist state and the Catholic Church. Once again he feels alienated from his natural critical social function. To criticize communist power is easy, but today intellectually sterile and without moral significance; to criticize the Church or the nation is for him morally (and politically) impossible. He is paralyzed by his previous experiences, by his individual and collective feelings of guilt. [This critical judgement of the 'guilt complex' of the Polish intelligentsia is not bound to diminish that group's crucial role in toppling the communist regime. It refers, rather, to the 'uneasy consciousness' of a social group that finds itself increasingly stripped of a 'historical mission'. Now, with a Solidarity-run government in Poland, and with a Catholic intellectual as Prime Minister, one can envision the advent of a new 'romantic' stage in the complicated historical itinerary of the Polish intellectuals. (Eds)]

Polish intellectuals are no longer united, and this is the second source of their frustration. The unity regained in the 1970s has broken down, although not yet dramatically, because different groups seek national salvation from different sources. Many of them, ready to negotiate with the authorities, continue to claim Solidarity's right to public existence and identify themselves with the social and political philosophy of this movement. Some, moral fundamentalists, refuse any compromise with communist power. For them, the only worthy objectives are independence and liberty, and the only politics possible today are the politics of moral integrity. Others look to the Church for space for independent collective action; still others espouse political realism and search for a compromise with communist government. There are also those who abandon the public sphere altogether and think that the only true treason of the *clerc* is the betrayal of his intellectual vocation.

These divisions reflect not only the crisis of the opposition after the defeat but also the feeling, cherished by some, that there are meaningful political choices now available. With this conviction coexists another, contradictory one, expressed by an official journalist: 'Today in Poland it is possible to say almost everything, but it is impossible to do almost anything'. Even if the conclusion is exaggerated and today's Poland is much more open than in the pre-Solidarity period, this sense of powerlessness is the third reason for the frustration of the Polish intellectual.

The situation of the Polish intellectual today is thus difficult. He shares most of his problems with the whole society, but some of them are his own, inherent in his natural condition as critic and rebel. Like everyone else, he doesn't know how to find a way out of the Polish stalemate, nor does he know a solution to his own dilemmas. Despite these frustrations, however, his problems sometimes seem secondary even to him. The prodigal son rejoices to have found his way home.

23 Cultural Dilemmas In Contemporary Bulgaria

Atanas Slavov

IDEOLOGICAL CULTURE

What Bulgarians cherish most about their culture is that, historically, it is one of ideological diversity and openness.

Although Bulgarians were dedicated East Orthodox Christians during the Middle Ages, their country was the cradle of the egalitarian Bogomil heresy. During this century, Bulgaria brought forward the small owner's movement of the Agrarian Union, and the mystical ideology of the 'have-nots' of the White Brotherhood, both of which have gained international significance.

As far as openness goes, Bulgarians, are proud that in the Middle Ages their ancestors were the first to announce that everyone should evolve spiritually according to his native cultural traditions. They broke the dogma of the three sacred languages: their scholars dared to translate the *Bible* into Slavic dialects and helped Kiev have a liturgy in its own tongue at the time when the British were still chanting it in Latin.

At the time of the building of the modern Bulgarian state, Bulgarian leaders broke with the imperializing dominance of Moscow just as they had broken with Constantinople during the Middle Ages. They started a feverish cultural reorientation toward the West. The leader of the liberals, Dragan Tsankov, even accepted the idea of a union with the Pope in order to diminish the Russian influence in the Orthodox Church. The constitution the Bulgarians adopted for their modern state was written along the lines of the liberal Belgian one, in a flagrant challenge to everything that authoritarian Russia stood for. Education and modernization were modeled exclusively along Western European liberal lines.

Breaking with Western values and liberalism and having an Eastern-style dictatorship imposed upon them during the days of Stalin have been a traumatic experience for the Bulgarian mind.

ECONOMIC CULTURE

The Bulgarians are pathetically industrious people longing to be up-to-date with the achievements of the world. During the days of the Ottoman reforms in the early nineteenth century, they were the ones to build the first textile factories in the Balkans and dress the modern Ottoman army.

In 1972 Taylor and Hudson's *World Handbook* showed Bulgaria already first in Eastern Europe in its pace of urbanization. In higher education, it was in eighth place in Europe. Bulgaria was ahead of the Soviet Union in all areas of communication and information: telephones (Bulgaria, 42nd place; USSR, 59th) media, including radio, TV and newspapers (Bulgaria, 33rd place; USSR, 41st). In 1975 statistics for the Balkans showed Bulgaria far ahead of all other Balkan countries in industrialization, with agriculture there being only 30 per cent of the entire national product. (For the second country, Romania, it was 40 per cent; for Greece, 40.6 per cent; and for Turkey, 65 per cent).

This was achieved not because of the imposed socialist culture but despite it, because of the traditional Bulgarian industriousness against all odds. Today, less than 20 per cent of the land belongs to private lots, which produce up to 40 per cent of the high-profit farm crops Bulgaria exports. Bulgaria was the first East European country after Yugoslavia to experiment with private economic initiatives, long before Hungary did. During Khrushchev's time, more than half of the residential construction in Bulgaria was private. Laws were passed in the USSR following the Bulgarian example, but the applications for private construction in Moscow were nil.

The Bulgarians feel there are strong differences between their own cultural tradition (a highly individualized, private, and enterprising ethos based on 13 centuries of experience of the free farmer who paid his taxes to medieval Bulgarian and Ottoman rulers in order to be left alone) and the similarly ancient tradition of the Russian serf (who fought not for a better chance for free enterprise but for a better ruler). The history of Russia is of social glory under efficient emperors (Ivan the Terrible, Peter the Great, Catherine). The entire history of Bulgaria is the history of flowering under a lenient central power (Joan Assen II, Boris III) and of devastating depression under strong, centralized power (Stamboliyski, Alexander Tsankov).

Following the traditions of their economic culture, Bulgarians strive for decentralization but are hindered by the stagnant socialist system that has been imposed upon them. An example: the data of the US Department of Commerce show that Bulgaria has a low foreign debt and good hard-currency resources, and is moving toward decentralization. Yet Bulgarians are still bound to the CMEA. In the spirit of perestroika the Soviets are now asking world-level prices for the energy they sell to Bulgaria, and expect world-market quality from the burdensome low-profit metallurgical enterprises they forced Bulgaria to build for their own strategic purposes during Stalin's days. Bulgaria has not been permitted to get out from under the burden of these extremely unprofitable metallurgical plants to dedicate itself to the high-profit industrial products for which it has been striving.

POLITICAL CULTURE

Reticent as the Bulgarians are, they do not believe (as Russians do) in noisily publicized campaigns, be they of dissent or otherwise. Dissenters, quite isolated from each other, silently work at preserving the last crumbs of their national traditions and resisting alien influence.

This has been an escalating process. In the 1970s, for the first time, high-ranking officials and party members who three decades earlier were instrumental in the communization of Bulgaria, voiced their doubts as to the soundness of their past actions. Those voices were the voices of despair, but, according to Western observers, because of traditional egalitarianism and introspectiveness Bulgarian dissidents appealing to world opinion are not likely to appear. In my comparative study of East European cultures for the Wilson Center (1979) I predicted that Bulgaria's resistance would not take the form of a politically organized dissident movement but of coups and acts of individual terrorism. In the early 1980s the first terrorist acts in Bulgaria were reported. Later they intensified in such a way that in 1985 a law was passed against terrorism. The nadir of national despair had been reached.

FAMILY CULTURE

Bulgarians have lost their pride and their hopes of reaching their cultural goals. The once sacred Bulgarian family used to starve to give a West European education and a financial start to its young ones. Now, after four decades of political indoctrination of its children in socialist public schools and failure to reach financial stability no matter how hard they worked, the Bulgarian family has given up its traditional dreams.

Why bring up children at all?' has become a common question young Bulgarians ask themselves. Bulgarians are dying out, and the minimal growth of the country's population is due to the high birth rates of Moslem Bulgarian citizens – Turks, Tartars and Gypsies. Before long Bulgaria will be a country with the ethnic Turks in the majority. They will move in on the grounds deserted by the Bulgarians who are committing ethnic suicide.

Bulgarians are aware of their predicament, and in the context of perestroika they are going to try any possibility that emerges in order to protect their cultural traditions. Voices from within Bulgaria and in the emigration in the West have called on Bulgarians to put aside their political differences and to pin down the spots in Bulgaria where resistance to the process of denationalization is taking place, supporting them from within and from without for the preservation of Bulgarian culture.

Like the East German rock fans behind the Berlin wall in the spring of 1987 who were chanting 'Gor-ba-chev!' while the police were clubbing them, Bulgarians will go for Gorbachev's reforms as long as they can see in them some hope of protecting what is left of their traditions – if the road to a Bulgarian Bulgaria led through hell they would follow it, chanting: 'Long live the Devil!' And Gorbachev is not the Devil. He is a reformist who will have to pay for the health of the 'sick man'. We will have to bargain. We have to make him pay with as much improvement and liberalization as possible for every step toward his goals, for he is the one in Eastern Europe who has the bread and holds the knife to slice it. Bulgarians who care believe that if ideological blindness (spelled 'impotence') leads them to ignore the possibilities that Gorbachev's compromise offers, history is not going to forgive them.

That is the way, I think, the Bulgarian nation is going to try to go as long as it is still on the map.

Our Czech friend Ivan Sviták, speaking of the Soviet regime, urged Western politicians and businessmen: 'Please, unplug the oxygen machine, and let the "sick man" die!' I am not a Prague alchemist. I am a vegetable grower from Tartar-Mezahr in Sliven, so let me try some vegetable images. There are a half a billion people there on that farm which covers one fourth of the land of this earth from Berlin to Kamchatka. If the 'sick man' dies, who is going to take over that farm, who is going to manage it? I am reading Solzhenitsyn and the Soviet dissidents, I am reading *Praxis* and Zinoviev, and I don't see who is going to take over. Only the Poles have claimed their future seriously, with the union between Solidarity and the Catholic Church. It is too early to speak of deaths. Even a good carrot needs almost three months to grow to full size. How long would it take for a new climate to ripen in the East and for the new ethics of an organized opposition to unfold? [It is fascinating to notice how difficult (and risky) political forecasting can be. After all, in November 1989, Bulgarians got rid of the old dictator Todor Zhivkov and embarked on the road to a multi-party system. But could one have predicted such developments even several months earlier? (Eds).]

The carrot has hardly shown a green shoot, and we shouldn't jump all over it and pull it to grow faster. Move aside! Give it the sun it needs, air, water! And a lot of natural fertilizer – but even dung needs time to ripen.

The dung is our past, and that is why I see the future in the past. We'll never grow to maturity if we have no chance to absorb our heritage through our new roots.

24 Civilization versus Anti-Civilization: To Graduate Or Not

Dorin Tudoran

Some consider valid the premise that the destructive and anti-cultural vocation of communism has been clear ever since its appearance. However, in his essay 'Communism as a Cultural Formation' (*Survey*, Summer 1985), Leszek Kolakowski raises the following query:

> How can we explain the fact that, given certain historical conditions, international communism, as a ruling ideology, and while aspiring to power, has proven so culturally fecund? In other words, how did it prove capable of inspiring works of art which should still be considered part of European civilization and which have at least not been consigned to the rubbish bin, and how did it manage to attract a considerable cross-section of the cultural élite, among them individuals of outstanding ability?

I find many of Kolakowski's conclusions acceptable, but it is precisely because I agree with so much that I admit my puzzlement at a curious choice of words: 'communist civilization'. He uses this strange phrase even though he calls communist civilization 'a separate form of civilization which devastated and still attempts to destroy Europe's cultural heritage'. In my opinion, communist culture has never managed to assume the shape of a civilization. I would even say that 'communist civilization' is a contradiction in terms.

Just as there used to be a Nazi culture, there is such a thing as a communist culture; but by the same token there cannot be a communist civilization, just as there never was a Nazi civilization. To me, a civilization can be compared to a graduation – it is the PhD of a culture. The history of mankind has witnessed numerous cultures but only a handful of civilizations. One of those cultures unable to attain the degree of maturity of a civilization is the communist one.

It is almost common knowledge that one of the ways in which a culture legitimizes itself is by its lack of awe toward power. However, in the case of communist culture everything seems to boil down to a question of dressage: it is a matter of who tames whom.

First, fright tamed the biological level. Then, censorship tamed fright. Finally, self-censorship tamed the creative author. Full circle. The cage erected is perfect. Fright made the railings; censorship put on the lock. Self-censorship gave the polishing touch to the entire construction. First a victim, the prisoner has acceded to a different status – that of an accomplice. The creative artist inside communist culture is not a tragic character given to self-illusion: he or she is a person who delights – either in public or secretly – in the relics offered by the establishment *qua* power; he or she is given to self-deceit and lies like that mythological shabby horse said to have eaten embers in order to gather force to break away from its predicament. Such a creator confuses freedom with its bookish representations. Such an artist generally refuses to acknowledge that the only cage which cannot be escaped is the cage whose railings are made of the prisoner's own bones and flesh. This indeed is the ideal kind of detention.

Thus, in the beginning was fright – it has exerted its narcotic effect on the place. Then came censorship – this was the bulldozer threatening the house. In recent times, self-censorship has become dominant. The latter is no longer a frightening bulldozer; it is the very foundation of the house... I mean, of the cage...

One of the common fallacies about communism is contained in a term which originally used to belong to economics. It is said that communism nationalizes things. Nothing could be more remote from the truth, especially in the realm of culture. Communism does not nationalize anything – it simply annihilates. Communist culture, for instance, doesn't belong to anybody: it doesn't belong to its creator, because he or she has every reason in the world to be doubtful about what it produces, both at the stage of censorship and at the stage of self-censorship; nor is such a culture the property of the consumer, as he or she is suspicious of all its compromises, even if having to do with its masterpieces. Communist culture doesn't belong to the state either, because the state simply tolerates it, even when, in fact, culture is subservient to the state and to its power and interests. One can not enjoy what one merely tolerates. And it is a very simple truth to demonstrate that everything that ever had any value in a communist system has, in fact, acted against power. Power, however, has tolerated heresy. That is how the three-fold lack of true possession was born: creator, consumer and the state being alike devoid of property in terms of culture, all three levels are, in fact, frustrated by such a culture which ends up by not belonging to anybody. This is exactly the opposite of nationalizing. . .

In order to achieve a superior stage – that of a civilization – a culture has to take at least three exams: that of Weltanschauung, that of a specific destiny and that of an axis mundi. Communist culture cannot attain the level of civilization for the simple reason that Fright can not be substituted for a Weltanschauung; Censorship cannot make up for a destiny; and self-censorship cannot build an axis mundi.

While trying to get from culture to civilization, which Kolakowski calls 'a cultural formation', communist culture broke down in a very specific manner. In that shipwreck the survivors, at least for the time being, and theoretically speaking, have had the chance to send a message in a bottle. We East Europeans throw it out to an ocean that keeps returning it to us, in an obstinate reverse move, right to the shore from whence it was thrown. However, a shipwreck culture is possible. The classical example is, of course, Robinson Crusoe. Defoe's character is portrayed in the process of building it up, bit by bit. Moreover, the character is apt to bring into play a foreigner – Friday. Yet shipwrecking is not likely to build up a civilization of its own. The best example is again Robinson Crusoe: after having worked out every possibility within reach, the character has to go; there is no room for further progress, no further step possible toward civilization. Crusoe's only chance is that of getting back to the one whose offspring he is.

So, what are the chances of a shipwrecked communist?

Hard to say. . .

In order to become a civilization, a culture needs a mythology. Lenin, Trotsky and Stalin were all well aware of this. Conversely, the mythology of that part of the world which preserves freedom as an axis mundi stems from a willingness to confer exponential power on that which is exceptional. So, against it the mythology of those who despise freedom is nothing but a collection of ghosts usurping the dignity of symbols. In 1848 Karl Marx would write in the opening page of his 'Manifesto' that 'a ghost' – as he put it – 'was wandering across Europe – Communism'. Now, on the threshold of the twenty-first century, Michel Heller, in a penetrating book entitled *Cogs in the Wheel: The Formation of the Soviet Man* (New York: Knopf, 1988) has reviewed the whole series of ghosts that followed the communist myths. That is the idea of any non-communist society as an inferno and the necessity to create a new world; the myths – and the mysteries – of revolution, of the state, the myth of an all-powerful and all-knowing party and that of its immortal leader; the myth of the monolith. None of them managed to round up identities of their own. All have started by biting into the antecedent myth and all ended in their own destruction by future myths. Thus the myth of the immortal leader took the place of the myth of the state, but that came to be ridiculed, as in Russia, by Khrushchev, who denounced the personality cult. To counter reality, communism has come up with gigantic chimeras. As a matter of fact, the fundamental error of communism is, in my view, that of confusing mythology with ideology. On a practical level, the disaster boils down to the attempt to produce on a conveyer belt that entity which prior utopias (those of Plato, Campanella, Morus, Münzer, Fourier, and others) only created as a simple archetype – the new man.

Mythology refuses the idea of serial achievement; ideology, on the contrary, cannot exist without such a standard. Even in decline, in that long twilight of which Spengler wrote ominously, the West remains a civilization. What separates it from communism in an essential way is a very simple matter, as described by Michel Heller:

Once freed from concentration camps by allies, many of the Soviet prisoners simply refused to go home. Over two million Soviet prisoners of war were turned over to Soviet authorities by British and Americans against their will. The Western allies had no way of understanding why these soldiers and officers freed from the Nazi camps would not return home. The older among them were fully aware that at best new camps were waiting for them at home. The British and American mentalities were simply incapable of realizing such facts. On the other hand, the Soviets were shocked to realize that the tens of thousands of Western servicemen, which they had freed from Nazi camps were being given hero welcomes in Britain, France and United States.

Nothing draws a sharper separation line than the perspective from which an onlooker considers, accepts or refuses liberty. In this connection it is interesting to note that psychiatrists believe that persons capable of simulating madness in the long run end up giving up simulation and become genuine madmen.

Can one become free by endlessly simulating freedom?

I, for one, can't believe it. And that is why I believe there is no such a thing as a communist civilization.

Nowhere else is this conflict more cogent than in Europe, a continent torn into two, precisely because of the different function assigned to liberty. This rift has created its own myths, its own utopias and all these face each other from opposite positions on the two sides of reality.

Myth stands on the right side of reality; on its left stands utopia. Myth spins a sweet story about 'old European unity'. Utopia whispers the seductive sirensong of 'regaining unity'. However, reality does not stand idly by; it passes before our eyes suggestive examples, one thousand years, several centuries or just a few hours old. And behold – the dirty cloak of Europe practicing cultural chauvinism, the thin lips of cultural arrogance; behold – the furrowed brow of cultural protectionism, the airs of cultural autarchy. The hymn of the political ghetto is 'Better red than dead!' The hymn of the cultural ghetto is 'Better de-Europeanized than non-existant!' Real-politik and Cultural-real-politik are but one and the same grimace of the cynicism of reality.

Politically, after World War II, Europe lost Mitteleuropa. Morally, it has lost rather its Western side. Culturally, it basks in perpetual convalescence.

We have become accustomed to visualizing a border as a river or a mountain, as a wall or as miles and miles of barbed wire. However, often the most ferocious border remains the cultural one. 'Mitteleuropa as a Cultural Border'? But, why not 'Western Europe as a Cultural Border'? In terms of this continent's destiny the two are perfectly synonymous. As in mathematics, the direction is the same, the magnitude is different.

We exhaust ourselves wondering whether we know what to say to each other or whether we have anything to say to one another at all. From time to time, to embolden ourselves, we furtively slip encouraging notes to each other, under the curtain, a curtain of iron today, of stone yesterday, of lasers tomorrow: 'Remember Antiquity!' 'Don't forget Christianity!' 'The Age of Enlightenment!' And yet coherence is just what the European cultural pedigree has always lacked.

Today Western Europe is a community of pre-utopian states; Middle and East Europe, one of post-utopian states. The former merely read Plato and More, Marx and Koestler, Campanella and Orwell. The latter have lived through these worlds, these Europes. And if myth can degenerate into a malignant lie, the danger of utopia is in its implementation, which can only be a caricature. Between these two types of experience, Europe is a cultural border in itself, for itself. The threatening sentry posts of this border are called self-disgust, self-defeat and self-sufficiency.

In their exile, Middle and East Europe abolished the myth of utopia. In its resignations, Western Europe nullified the utopia of myth. We have become accustomed to living with diabetes. We are learning to live with cancer. But what else is culture if not the only chance to survive creatively, for the time being, with our irreversible amputations, on the road to choose our destiny creatively?

There is a species of bird whose members are endowed with only one wing, either the left or right one. When such a bird wishes to fulfill its destiny – that is, to fly – a right-winged bird joins a left-winged one. The spectacle of such a flight is extraordinary, bordering on the tragic. When such a bird is content to crawl on the ground it does not cross the borders of melodrama.

Because I can't remember the name of this bird, and I don't

have time to look it up in a specialized dictionary, I call it Europe.

Getting back to Leszek Kolakowski's essay, let me say that I fully endorse the philosopher's observation that 'Communism has been a gigantic façade'. I would even say that nothing was better achieved by communism than the flabbergasting multiplication of pasteboard façades of the Potemkin type – the tzar's Count being from that viewpoint a Communist *avant la lettre*.

While still a fearful force in terms of power, communism has proved to be an immensely tragic farce on a political level. Philosophically speaking, it has been nothing but a cacophony.

In terms of pathology I would say that its advent into history has all the features of the delirium tremens of this century.

As a civilization, however, communism was born dead.

Let me dwell for a moment on a paradox. The chance of talent in the case of artists born in today's part of Europe resides here: since there is no communist civilization, the achievements of such artists can not belong to it. Their accomplishments belong, in fact, to the civilization of Europe. This is indeed a strange artistic destiny to which communism has given unwitting birth.

Some might feel like asking me the following question: 'When did you come to get an understanding of all this?'

My answer is simple. It all happened at the exact time that someone made bold to give me one of the few real truths of communism, and I quote: 'Comrade Tudoran, try to be careful. We are the ones who can kill you, and no one else but ourselves are the ones who can rehabilitate you.'

On hearing that I realized what absolute captivity is like. There was nothing left for me to do but to take my leave, shun the challenge and become an exile. As far as exile is concerned, it can be a form of civilization or one of the forms of suicide.

About a century ago, William James wrote: 'The problem with man is less what act he shall now choose to do, than what being he shall now resolve to become.'

Such a thought gets one back into the sphere of civilization any time.

25 Bitter Love: Chinese Intellectuals and the State

Judith Shapiro

Chinese intellectuals are born to a bitter love. They feel a deep responsibility to 'make a contribution' to their long-troubled and beloved motherland, knowing clearly that they may well end up devoured or broken, having sacrificed their lives to a futility. This is an ancient tradition: Chinese intellectuals have been throwing themselves into metaphorical rivers ever since Qu Yuan, China's first poet, drowned himself in the Xiang out of patriotic devotion. The reformers of today are the direct heirs of those who died trying to reform China during the Hundred Days' Reform of 1898 and the May Fourth movement of 1919.

Chinese intellectuals today swing between shame at what they see as China's inferiority before the world, and pride or even arrogance over memories of greatness past. There is a kind of obsession with the nation's 'face' that reveals the pain of lost cultural and political superiority; there is often a sense of rueful surprise, as if this former glory had been somehow mislaid when everyone's back was turned. Some say the decline occurred during the Mao era, when China sealed its doors against the outside world, all the while congratulating itself on its own near-suicidal social experiments; only when the doors reopened did the extent of the self-delusion become apparent. Nearly every Chinese intellectual has his theories about China's 'backwardness', and most of them confront the issue as if it were a personal one. They are preoccupied with arcane debates as to whether Confucianism is a feudal philosophical system that has held China back from modernity, or a rich moral tradition with a strong message for a nation gripped by a crisis of values; they argue about their educational system, and why it has failed to produce the scientific breakthroughs for which China has been historically famous.

Chinese intellectuals often describe their own deep patriotism as a 'bitter love' (*kulian*), a reference to the famous movie script of the same name by the army film studio writer Bai Hua. The target of a 1981 campaign against 'bourgeois liberalism', the script told the all-too-common story of an overseas Chinese artist who returns to help his country, only to be 'persecuted to death' during the 1957 anti-rightist movement. The question mark his last footsteps leave in the snow punctuates the film's central (and most heavily-criticized) cry of agony: 'You love the motherland, but does the motherland love you?'

The love is bitter not only because it is often unrequited but also because it cannot be renounced. Chinese intellectuals are destined to it, as to a fate. It is a source of continuous conflict and torment. Yet although they wrestle with it, few can give it up. As students and visiting scholars in the West, they envy other foreigners who arrive with simpler moral baggage, and they half wish that they could exorcise their sense of duty and remain here to pursue personal goals. Those who do elect to stay usually bear a heavy load of guilt, often rationalizing their decisions with the thought that they can do more for China from outside, working to strengthen China's ties with the West and explore alternatives to the Soviet model. Others tell themselves that they will return to China after they have their resident alien cards or US citizenships. Even those who have been in the West for most of their lives often try to find ways of making a contribution through investments, trade or stints as teachers. The desire to find solutions to China's ills is infectious: many if not all Western visitors are touched by China's struggles and filled with a desire to 'help'; some dedicate years or even lifetimes to China's cause.

One source of many Chinese intellectuals' ambivalence is their reluctant acceptance of the notion that such personal freedoms as freedom of movement or choice of residence and occupation must remain limited for the foreseeable future (not to speak of freedom to reproduce – most educated Chinese fully accept the one-child family policy as an essential, necessary evil). Even such aspects of free expression as artistic freedom and freedom of the press are often conceded to be luxuries that cannot be afforded by a country too continually close to chaos for potentially destabilizing ideas to be promoted freely. There is a common belief that the Chinese people are so 'backward' that they need restrictions, that society's goods are too scarce to be decontrolled, and that if free elections were held, a dictator would be chosen. Despite some highly limited improvements in personal and intellectual freedoms, most Chinese intellectuals seem to believe that the democratic, free-thinking, artistically sophisticated China in which they themselves would prefer to live is an impossible dream, just as they have come to accept that their own political roles will probably always be sharply circumscribed.

Although it is a common Western assumption that educated people are a force for democracy and political pluralism, in China this is not always true. One major reason is that long-standing Chinese cultural traditions stress a fundamental harmony of interests between ruler and ruled. The ancient view is that it is the duty of an intellectual to make constructive criticisms of the existing regime, but not to challenge its fundamental authority. As the word is used in Chinese, 'democracy' generally means the right to air opinions so that rulers can become better rulers. Contemporary distinctions between 'bourgeois democracy' and 'socialist democracy' are such that Chinese may consider their society democratic when its leaders serve their interests well. Even political activists, from the 1978–79 Democracy Wall movement poets and writers to the 1987 student demonstrators, tend to see themselves as enlisting on the side of a faction within the regime. Many of those whom Westerners have wanted to label dissidents are acutely uncomfortable with the appellation, preferring to call themselves patriots or true Marxists. Given this cultural context, Leninist centralism is best seen as a foreign import congruent with local conditions; it reenforced rather than overturned entrenched feudal and bureaucratic traditions.

For thousands of years in China there has been a deeply-held belief that the emperor cannot be wrong: if there is misrule, it is supposed that this is because he is surrounded by corrupt officials who are misinforming him, blocking the lines of communication between him and the people. Traditionally, the hierarchy could be circumvented through the use of 'memorials to the emperor'. Mao appealed to the feudalistic loyalty to the emperor when he publicized the Cultural Revolution as an opportunity for the masses to defend him against his enemies: in fact, he had become engaged in a power struggle against those critical of his disastrous late 1950s experiments with too-rapid communalization and industrialization. After the revolution the same loyalty to the top leader made it possible for party officials afraid of shaking the foundations of their authority to displace the anger at Mao onto 'the Gang of Four'. Today it is entirely consistent with tradition that in a remote cave area a peasant, bemoaning the abuses he suffers at the hands of local officials, listens to the voice of Deng Xiaoping on the radio and says sadly, 'I can hear Old Deng but he cannot hear me'.

Another reason that Chinese intellectuals are not always a force for greater political democracy is their painful memories of their still-recent victimizations during the Cultural Revolution. Especially among older intellectuals, the desire for freedom *from* political movements, chaos and persecution is greater than the desire for freedom and democracy. Hence the students who demonstrated in the streets of Shanghai in early 1987 enjoyed little popular support, even from other intellectuals: while many were sympathetic to the students' goals of greater freedom of speech and political participation, they were terrified that their means would bring about a backlash by orthodox hard-liners and put an end to the relaxations of social controls that have accompanied the new economic freedoms. The June 1989 Tienanmen events proved these cautions were justified.

A statement from the old dramatist Xia Yan, an influential arts official, is revealing of traditional intellectuals' emphasis on the harmony of goals between themselves and the state: 'I was imprisoned for eight years and forced to write nearly a thousand confessions. I need not mention the beatings and personal insults I suffered. A foreign friend suggested that I describe these experiences, but as a party member and a patriot, I felt that I should not. To reveal that fascism is still strong in China could frighten the people. We must not follow in the steps of a certain writer from the Soviet Union who specialized in writing about prison camps and went to Western countries to publish his works. This course of action does not benefit the Chinese people, nor does it strengthen our unity and stability'. Xia Yan's lack of anger at what he suffered is typical of older Chinese intellectuals, and can perhaps be explained only in the context of ancient traditions.

Despite their recent terrible humiliations in the dregs of society, intellectuals in China today are among society's blessed. Where Mao said, 'the more books you read, the more foolish you become', the rehabilitation of intellectuals was one of Deng Xiaoping's priorities after his return to power in 1977. Deng's emphasis on the importance of intellectuals is one of the three cornerstones of his modernization campaign, together with the opening to the outside world and the 'enlivening of the economy'. From their Mao-era categorization as members of the 'stinking ninth', intellectuals have been elevated to what one middle school teacher jokingly but also fearfully called the 'fragrant first'. They have been redefined as 'mental workers' and given an array of privileges that for 'high intellectuals' can mean huge apartments, private cars and drivers, special ration coupons and some of the greatest job mobility currently available to government employees. They have been encouraged to join the party (as recently as ten years ago, two-thirds of party members had a primary school education or less) and to voice their opinions about reform from within. They have been promoted to leading managerial and policy-making positions, while their poorly-educated predecessors have been bumped into 'advisory' posts where their party functions are now officially isolated from administrative influence.

However, Chinese intellectuals are still cautious about their new situations. Many are well aware that the current high status of intellectuals, with the concurrent national fetish about examinations and diplomas, is consistent with thousands of years of feudal hyper-awareness of rank and hierarchy. They have not forgotten that in its original impulse the Cultural Revolution was a highly democratic mass movement that derived much of its strength from resentment toward groups with privileges similar to those that have been restored to them today. They remember how disenfranchised ordinary Chinese with long-suppressed grievances seized the opportunity to level social hierarchies and attack the arrogant and privileged cadres within the party, propaganda and arts units and educational system; only later, as the revolution twisted out of control and the human sacrifices became overwhelming did the rebels understand that they had been used.

Despite the popular support for the reforms, intellectuals who have suffered before are afraid that they may suffer again: cycles of privilege, envy and revenge remain latent cultural patterns in China. While Chinese bemoan this, they cannot seem to free themselves of it: neighbors (jokingly called victims of 'the red eye disease') keep a jealous eye on each other as if waiting for the opportunity to 'climb up the backs of others' in their own pursuit of privilege. In this nation of scarcity, Chinese say, people cannot seem to save themselves without pushing others down into the muck. However, intellectuals are less deeply resented today than are the sons and daughters of high party leaders, who use their immunity from normal constraints to go abroad to study and profiteer in domestic and international business in violation of official regulations.

Cultural and philosophical traditions that emphasize hierarchical order, social stability and obedience to authority are thus still very much alive in China. It is primarily among younger, less experienced intellectuals that there is a push toward rapid democratization in the Western sense, and even among these activists there is a strong belief that without major changes in the economic and cultural foundations of society, fundamental political reforms will be impossible. What these younger activists share with their elders is the heritage of all Chinese intellectuals: a bitter love for their country, foredoomed, perhaps, to expend itself on lifelong efforts that bear only short-lived fruit.

26 Dialectics of Disenchantment

Vladimir Tismaneanu

For decades, Communist ideology has played the role of substitute for religious symbols and values. Several generations have come to political age by assimilating a radical promise of universal redemption and emancipation.

The ethos of Christianity was challenged by Marxist pretense. Morality was defined in terms of loyalty to a sense of ultimate historical transcendance. First Leninism, then Stalinism codified this total commitment to an apocalyptic scenario dedicated to bringing about not only a new type of society but also a new type of person. With its ambition to initiate an anthropological revolution, Marxism can be regarded as a form of utopian radicalism: utopian because it is basically future-oriented and overlooks the perennial features of the human condition; radical inasmuch as it aims to transform the body politic and establish a form of social organization totally different from all previous ones.

Conceived by its founding fathers as an anti-statist philosophy, Marxism has culminated in the Soviet apotheosis of the party and state machine. Under Lenin and Stalin, ideology represented a major source of power for communist élites. The legitimacy of the Bolshevik élite derived primarily from its relationship to the Marxist doctrine. Arcane as they sounded to external observers, the squabbles of the 1920s touched on the most sensitive points of what Czeslaw Milosz has called the New Faith, an ideology 'based on the principle that good and evil are definable solely in terms of service or harm to the interests of the Revolution'.[1]

At least throughout the first decade of the new revolutionary regime people were enthusiastically ready to espouse Leninist dogma. The social promises and revolutionary spirit of Bolshevism were invoked as arguments against those who deplored the violence generated by dictatorial power. Many intellectuals, including some famous names like Maxim

Gorky, André Gide, Arthur Koestler, Manès Sperber, Romain Rolland, André Malraux and Ignazio Silone, were fascinated by what seemed to be a heroic historical adventure. Some of them grew disappointed with the cynicism of the communist commisars and left the Leninist chapels; others, like Pablo Neruda or Louis Aragon, refused to abjure their faith and remained attached to hackneyed communist tenets.

The Short Course of History of the CPSU, published in 1938, represented the paradigm of Bolshevik intellectual debasement. Turned into a gospel for the international communist movement, this parody of Marxism was extolled as the pinnacle of human wisdom. After the occupation of East-Central Europe by the USSR, the same form of primitive Leninism – they never dared to call it Stalinism – was decreed the unique interpretation of true Marxism. In 1948 Tito was excommunicated and Titoism branded a form of ideological infiltration by the enemy into the revolutionary camp. a diabolical 'fifth column' fomenting subversion and sowing discord. In the communist countries, the mind agonized in the captivity of the thought police.

But things started to move again after Nikita Khrushchev's fulminating attack on Stalinism at the 20th Congress of the CPSU in February 1956. Khrushchev's outstanding courage in launching the onslaught against the prevailing communist orthodoxy is now recognized by official Soviet ideologues. One of the most interesting attempts to rehabilitate Khrushchev was recently published by Fyodor Burlatsky, a noted Soviet political commentator and one of Gorbachev's close advisors. In many respects, Burlatsky's assessment echoes the judgment on Khrushchevism formulated by revisionist authors of the 1960s. He sees one of Khrushchev's cardinal weaknesses in the fact that 'the quest for a prospectus for reforms and means of implementing them was based on traditional administrative and even bureaucratic methods'.[2] As we see, the myth-breaking assault on the Stalinist interpretation of Marxism was launched by intellectuals with deep links to Communist political culture.

'Revisionism', a term coined by neo-Stalinist orthodoxies to stigmatize critical currents of thought, has been the main adversary encountered by ruling bureaucrats since the factional struggles of the mid and late 1920s. The yearning

for a moral reform of communism was the basic motivation
for the neo-Marxist revivalism in Eastern Europe following
Stalin's death; the intellectuals' rebellion against totalitarian
controls has been one of the major threats experienced by
Soviet-type regimes. This has been true not only in Poland,
Hungary, Yugoslavia and Czechoslovakia, but also in the
Soviet Union, China, the GDR and Romania. The dubious
legitimacy of these governments was questioned by critics
who could not be accused of belonging to the defeated social
classes. With their outspoken advocacy of humanism and
democracy, they contributed to the erosion of the apparent
monolithic consensus.

In communist societies intellectuals oscillate between complicity with and resistance to power. Many have chosen the
first alternative because it does not involve any risk. Others
have imagined ways to escape the ideological mirage and
embarked on a long-term struggle for mental and political
autonomy. This relentless struggle for intellectual emancipation was inaugurated by the Petofi Circle in Hungary, the
neo-Marxist groups and journals in Poland and Czechoslovakia, and those Soviet writers who announced that man
does not live 'by bread alone'. But revisionism was nearly
suppressed because of its own commitment to values fatally
perverted through official manipulation. It was a fallacious
strategy based on wishful thinking and impossible desiderata
of moral regeneration of the ruling élite. It foolishly yearned
for dialogue with those who valued only brutal force. Adam
Michnik aptly describes the inescapable dilemma of neo-
Marxist revisionism in East-Central Europe: 'The revisionist
concept was based on a specific intraparty perspective. It
was never formulated into a political program. It assumed
that the system of power could be humanized and democ-
ratized and that the official Marxist doctrine was capable
of assimilating contemporary arts and social sciences. The
revisionists wanted to act within the framework of the Communist party and Marxist doctrine. They wanted to transform
"from within" the doctrine and the party in the direction of
democratic reform and common sense'.[3]

Communist domination relies upon social inertia, widespread contempt for politics and moral pessimism. Since
the early stage of communism, when historical romanticism

was inculcated into the masses, the system has been unable to inspire and mobilize large groups. Those who live under communism know that it is ethically decrepit and intellectually extinguished. Vladimir Bukovsky once said that the first genuine communists he ever met were those he encountered after he left the Soviet Union. To be sure, there are many socialist idealists in the Soviet bloc, but their views represent the antithesis of orthodox Leninism.

In the Russian tradition of reforms from above, Gorbachev's attempt to restore the moral impetus of communism is based on a miscalculation: as long as society is maintained under control, as long as civic independent initiatives can be legally repressed, the politics of glasnost will not acquire credibility. The need for a dramatic divorce from the past is recognized by the most radical partisans of perestroika. The 'Declaration of Moscow Conference of Socialist Clubs' issued in August 1987 formulates the following demands: legal status for independent organizations and associations; the granting to them of the right to initiate legislation and to secure the fulfillment of party decisions aimed at democratizing the electoral system; the granting of the right to social organizations to nominate their own representatives to all levels of the Soviets of People's Deputies without restrictions and in accord with free access of candidates to the mass media; establishment in law of a sharp distinction between criticism of the shortcomings of the existing system and anti-state activity; and realization of the first point of the program of the Russian Social-Democratic Labor Party concerning the rights of citizens to prosecute in court officials responsible for illegal acts, independent of complaints made at administrative levels.[4]

In every society man needs a set of guiding values whose observance promises to ensure his tranquillity and worldly achievements. Soviet-type regimes ignore this and force the individual to divide his soul between the public and private person. Man and citizen are different entities in these societies. What one says and what one thinks do not coincide most of the time. Institutional and family socialization therefore become divergent processes. Parents urge their children to conceal from friends and teachers what they hear at home. Teachers convey political messages they do not believe in. Apparatchiks applaud a general secretary they hate. Judges are politically appointed and the justice they render is, as the communist jargon goes, 'class-determined'. Political imagination and historical curiosity are discouraged by both school and family.

The outcome of this is apathy, general disgust with politics, drug addiction, interest in exotic cults or even fascination with Nazism, as in the case of certain Soviet youth groups. One can therefore regard the extinction of mystical ardor as a major liability of communist political systems. These systems experience a perpetual ideological crisis: their promises have long ago lost any credibility. Gorbachev's injunctions receive only lukewarm support from those he wishes to mobilize; party calls for innovation fail to galvanize social energies.

The glasnost campaign notwithstanding, very few things have changed in the structure of the propaganda ritual. The general secretary is still the only voice authorized to express the revealed truth. Ten years ago Leonid Brezhnev was a celebrated political personality and an alleged author of literary masterpieces. Nowadays, his name is almost completely forgotten. Tomorrow, if Gorbachev is ousted, his name will be thrown into oblivion too. The limits of the discussion and the scope and objectives of openness are prescribed by the ideological nomenklatura. It is hard to believe that Gorbachev and his supporters will transcend the limits of an updated, more sophisticated Khrushchevism: their mental horizon is determined by their attachment to the existing system. Change, including ideological reform, will not modify deeply entrenched prejudices, animosities, resentments and anguishes.

The ruling élites in communist countries cannot give in to calls for pluralism. The principal function of communist bureaucracy is to exert dictatorship over mind and body. The communist bureaucratic ethos involves a strong *esprit de corps*, a solidarity developed through common existential experience, continued paternalistic behavior and a jealously guarded monopoly of power. Agnes Heller and Ferenc Fehér are right when they write that Gorbachev cannot create institutional frameworks capable of perpetuating the modernizing momentum even if it can be set in motion: 'Gorbachev is truly an heir to the worst illusion of the Khrushchev era. He too keeps squaring the circle, reducing what is a major social and

political dilemma to the level of a mere technical problem. . .
For "modernization" to break through, politics cannot remain
a mere maidservant of technology'.[5]

The dissolution of civil society and the preservation of
atomized social space, the *sine qua non* of Soviet-type totalitarianism, have engendered widespread moral indifference and
intellectual corruption. The official language is second nature,
a protective shield against outbursts of spontaneity. People
simulate loyalty to the system, but this is ritualistic behavior
rather than sentimental attachment. As Vaclav Havel put it:
'Because of this dictatorship of the ritual, however, power
becomes anonymous. Individuals are almost dissolved in the
ritual. They allow themselves to be swept along by it and
frequently it seems as though ritual alone carries people from
obscurity into the light of power. . . The automatic operation
of a power structure thus dehumanized and made anonymous
is a feature of the fundamental automatism of this system'.[6]

Citizens of socialist countries have become master practi-
tioners of double-talk and double-think. The life of the mind
is split and the result of this excruciating process is that
not even the Soviet general secretary is entirely convinced
of what the party proclaims. Ideology functions more as a
residual institution than as a source of mystical identification
with the powers-that-be. Since the CPSU 20th Congress and
the Hungarian revolution, official slogans sound like a succession of senseless sentences. The only effect of ideological
sermonizing is an immense, all-pervasive ennui. Ironically,
ideological imperialism has resulted in a simulacrum of faith
which is merely a camouflage for the ideological vacuum. At
the moment this imposture is exposed the whole castle falls
apart. In Havel's words: '. . . ideology, as that instrument of
internal communication which assures the power structure of
inner cohesion is, in the post-totalitarian system, something
that transcends the physical aspects of power, something that
dominates it to a considerable degree and, therefore, tends
to assure its continuity as well. It is one of the pillars of the
system's external stability. This pillar, however, is built on a
very unstable foundation. It is built on lies. It works only as
long as people are willing to live within the lie'.[7]

Revisionist intellectuals who have done so much to subvert
the ideological façade of these regimes have abandoned their

illusions about the reformability of the system from within the ruling party. They want to rediscover the virtues of dialogue and the advantages of civilized discourse.

Members of the democratic opposition advocate the need to create an alternative form of politics. Hungarian writer George Konrád speaks of the emergence of antipolitics as a challenge to the apocryphal version of politics embodied by the system: 'The ideology of the democratic opposition shares with religion a belief that the dignity of the individual personality (in both oneself and the other person) is a fundamental value not requiring any further demonstration. The autonomy and solidarity of human beings are the two basic and mutually complementary values to which the democratic movement relates other values'.[8]

Bitter experiences in Poland, Hungary and Czechoslovakia have convinced these critics that the crux of the matter is to go beyond the logic of the system. There is no doubt that revisionism greatly contributed to putting an end to Marxist-Leninist self-satisfaction, but a main weakness of this orientation was its submission to the rules dictated by officialdom. For radical opponents of totalitarianism, revisionists looked like half-hearted allies; for ideological zealots, they were dangerous heretics. Their writings were esoteric, with little appeal to the large public. Moreover, their criticism was still encoded in the language of power.

On the other hand, the revisionist ideas of the 1960s catalyzed the emergence of a dissident counterculture. Disenchantment with Marxism was an opportunity to re-think the radical legacy and reassess the commitment to the Jacobin ideals of total community. In the struggle between the state and civil society, it was the latter's chance and task to invent a new principle of power that would hold in deep respect the rights and aspirations of the individual. This counter-principle was rooted in the independent life of society, in what Vaclav Havel, the Czech playwright and Charter 77 activist, now President of Czechoslovakia, aptly called the power of the powerless.

It has become increasingly important to debunk the duplicitous infrastructure of communist power. First Solzhenitsyn, then East and Central European dissidents announced their decision to restore the normative value of truth. Refusing official lies and reinstating truth in its own right has turned out to be a more successful strategy than the revisionist criticism from within.

It is now obvious that the main strength of communist regimes is their ability to maintain a climate of fear and hopelessness; their main weakness is the failure to muzzle the human mind. I do not underestimate the intrinsic economic problems of those regimes, but the principal source of instability lies in their failure to generate confidence. Even now, in the Soviet Union, people distrust Gorbachev's pledge of democratization, not because communist regimes are immutable or because there is nothing relevant occuring in the Soviet Union. But even those who are most optimistic about the current changes, including advocates of liberalization like Andrey Voznesenskiy, Vitaliy Korotich and Bulat Okudzhava, admit that the thaw is still superficial. Soviet cultural magazines may now be among the most exciting in the communist world, but they are still directed by the party's ideological department. The editorial plans have to be approved by party officials whose only credentials consist of unflinching obedience. Aleksandr Yakovlev, the alleged protector of the Soviet liberal intelligentsia, is a seasoned propaganda activist. No one should deny the astuteness of Gorbachev's strategy, but it would be naive to take it for anything but an effort to eliminate the most obnoxious features of ideological orthodoxy.

The Hungarian dissident philosopher Gaspar Miklós Támás expresses a widespread feeling among East European independents when he refuses to consider Gorbachevism as a godsend: 'I don't agree. . . with the complacency of most Western observers, especially now with the advent of Gorbachev, who would confine us within the limits of a mildly reformed communist system where the power still lies with the Party, but where some other people can also shout a bit. If people don't have to suffer for their views but nevertheless have no real influence over what happens, the longer such a situation continues the greater the difference develops between words and deeds. We cannot develop a normal life for the future on such a basis'.[9]

Of course, the ideological relaxation has indeed had disruptive effects not only in the Soviet Union, but also in East and Central Europe. It has permitted a redistribution of the constellation of power as a consequence of social self-organization. The experience of KOR in Poland has demonstrated that a tiny nucleus of committed intellectuals can fundamentally change the post-totalitarian political equation.[10] KOR contributed to the creation of climate of cooperation between the radical core of the intelligentsia and the militant activists of the working class. Neither a political party nor a traditional trade union, Solidarnosc prefigures a synthesis of non-utopian longings for a rational polis and an emancipated community.

Intellectuals in those countries know that the pace of reforms in the Soviet Union is of vital importance for the fate of East European nations. The intensification of dissident activities in the last two years in Poland, Hungary, Czechoslovakia and the GDR suggests that this is a propitious time for daring challenges to the regimes. The October 1986 statement signed by dissidents from Poland, Hungary, Czechoslavakia and the GDR inaugurated a new chapter in the history of anti-totalitarian struggles. It shows that international actions can and should be undertaken to emphasize the values and the goals of the opposition. [There is no doubt that critical intellectuals have been at the center of the epoch-making changes in Eastern Europe. Vaclav Havel's paramount role in the Czechoslovakia revolution in November 1989 (both as its symbol and its strategist) suggests that the intelligentsia will be more than a spectator in the reconstruction of political life during the years to come. The same can be said about the leaders of the Alliance of Free Democrats in Hungary, the members of the Group for Social Dialogue in Romania, the activists of *Ecoglasnost* in Bulgaria, the Polish opposition leaders turned members of the government or the Inter-Regional group in the Congress of People's Deputies in Moscow. It is now obvious that intellectuals have decisively contributed to the reconstitution of civil society and thereby to the disintegration of totalitarianism. (Eds)]

To conclude, communist regimes are more ideologically vulnerable than ever, and since ideology and power are inextricably linked in the nature of communist systems, increased social conflicts are to be expected in the countries of the Soviet empire. Against opposition actions and programs, the rulers cannot offer more than unfulfillable promises;

whenever this tactic does not work, they resort to naked violence. But the rise of independent social movements in East-Central Europe is a forceful indication of these systems' incapacity to domesticate their critics. As for glasnost, it is an attempt to solve the insoluble, a desperate endeavor to create a less suffocating environment without changing the principle of party domination. The fabric is perhaps softer, but the straitjacket has remained unchanged. As Miklós Haraszti put it in the afterword to the American edition of his book on artists under state socialism: '. . . for decades Hungary has been a textbook model for a pacified post-Stalinist neo-colony. This fact has not been lost on Mr. Gorbachev as he attempts to wrap more velvet on the bars of his prison in order to create a less primitive and more manageable order in the heart of his empire'.[11] It is the historical calling of critical intellectuals to counter the strategy of co-optation and assert the primacy of those values the system stifles. At the moment in which genuine independent social movements coalesce, intellectuals can provide an articulate program for political change. Thanks to critical intellectuals, revolts can become revolutions.

NOTES

1. See Czeslaw Milosz, *The Captive Mind* (New York: Vintage Books, 1981), p. 75.
2. See Fyodor Burlatsky, 'Khrushchev: Sketches for a Political Portrait', *Literaturnaya Gazeta*, 24 February 1988, p. 14.
3. See Adam Michnik, *Letters From Prison and Other Essays* (Berkeley: University of California Press, 1985), p. 135.
4. See *Labour Focus on Eastern Europe*, Vol. 9, No. 3, November 1987–February 1988, pp. 5–6.
5. See Agnes Heller and Ferenc Fehér, 'Khrushchev and Gorbachev: A Contrast', *Dissent*, Winter 1988, p. 10.
6. See Vaclav Havel *et al.*, *The Power of the Powerless: Citizens against state in central-eastern Europe* (Armonk, N.Y.: M.E. Sharpe, 1985), pp. 33–4.
7. Ibid., p. 35.
8. See George Konrád, *Antipolitics* (San Diego: Harcourt Brace Jovanovich, 1984), p. 123.
9. See 'There's More to Politics Than Human Rights', an interview with Gaspar Miklós Támás *Uncaptive Minds*, Vol. 1, No. 1, April–May 1988, p. 12.

10. See Jan Josef Lipski, *KOR: A History of the Workers' Defense Committee 1976–1981* (Berkeley: University of California Press, 1985).
11. See Miklos Haraszti, *The Velvet Prison: Artist Under State Socialism* (New York: Basic Books, 1987).

Index

222   *Index*